SIMON BLOCK

Simon Block was born and still lives in North London. He was educated in London, and then Southampton and Cambridge Universities. His theatre credits include *Not a Game for Boys* (Royal Court Theatre, 1995); *Chimps* and *No Exp. Req'd* (both Hampstead Theatre, 1997 and 1999 respectively) and *A Place at the Table* (Bush Theatre, 2000). His writing for television includes *Attachments* (BBC-2, 2001/2002); *North Square* (Channel Four, 2000) and *Safe as Houses* (ITV, 2000). He is married with two sons.

Also in this series

Patrick Barlow
LOVE UPON THE THRONE
THE MESSIAH
THE WONDER OF SEX

Simon Block
CHIMPS
NOT A GAME FOR BOYS
A PLACE AT THE TABLE

Caryl Churchill
BLUE HEART
CHURCHILL PLAYS: THREE
CHURCHILL: SHORTS
CLOUD NINE
FAR AWAY
HOTEL
ICECREAM
LIGHT SHINING IN
  BUCKINGHAMSHIRE
MAD FOREST
THE SKRIKER
THIS IS A CHAIR
THYESTES
TRAPS

David Edgar
ALBERT SPEER
DR JEKYLL AND MR HYDE
EDGAR: SHORTS
PENTECOST
THE PRISONER'S DILEMMA
THE SHAPE OF THE TABLE

Helen Edmundson
ANNA KARENINA
THE CLEARING
THE MILL ON THE FLOSS
WAR AND PEACE

Marie Jones
STONES IN HIS POCKETS

Mike Leigh
ECSTASY
SMELLING A RAT

Liz Lochhead
MEDEA (after Euripides)
MISERY GUTS
PERFECT DAYS

Clare McIntyre
MY HEART'S A SUITCASE
  & LOW LEVEL PANIC
THE THICKNESS OF SKIN

Conor McPherson
DUBLIN CAROL
MCPHERSON: FOUR PLAYS
PORT AUTHORITY
THE WEIR

Peter Nichols
PASSION PLAY
SO LONG LIFE

Terence Rattigan
AFTER THE DANCE
THE BROWNING VERSION
THE DEEP BLUE SEA
FRENCH WITHOUT TEARS
IN PRAISE OF LOVE
SEPARATE TABLES
THE WINSLOW BOY

Morna Regan
MIDDEN

Diane Samuels
KINDERTRANSPORT
THE TRUE LIFE FICTION
  OF MATA HARI

Sophie Treadwell
MACHINAL

Nicholas Wright
CRESSIDA
MRS KLEIN
VINCENT IN BRIXTON
WRIGHT: FIVE PLAYS

Simon Block

HAND IN HAND

NICK HERN BOOKS
London
www.nickhernbooks.co.uk

A Nick Hern Book

Hand in Hand first published in Great Britain in 2002
as a paperback original by Nick Hern Books Limited,
14 Larden Road, London W3 7ST

Hand in Hand copyright © 2002 Simon Block

Simon Block has asserted his right to be identified as the author of this work

Cover design: Ned Hoste, 2H

Typeset by Country Setting, Kingsdown, Kent CT14 8ES

Printed by LSL Press, Bedford, MK41 0TX

ISBN 1 85459 685 3

A CIP catalogue record for this book is available from the British Library

CAUTION   All rights whatsoever in this play are strictly reserved. Requests to reproduce the text in whole or in part should be addressed to the publisher

Amateur Performing Rights   Applications for performance, including readings and excerpts, in the English language throughout the world by amateurs (including stock companies in the United States of America and Canada) should be made before rehearsals begin to Nick Hern Books, 14 Larden Road, London W3 7ST, *fax* +44 (0) 208 735 0250; *e-mail* info@nickhernbooks.demon.co.uk

Professional Performing Rights   Applications for performance by professionals in any medium and in any language throughout the world (except for stock companies in the United States of America and Canada: see above) should be addressed to International Creative Management Ltd, 76 Oxford Street, London W1N 0AX

No performance of any kind may be given unless a licence has been obtained. Applications should be made before rehearsals begin. Publication of this play does not necessarily indicate its availability for amateur performance.

Hand in Hand was first staged on 14 February 2002 at Hampstead Theatre, London. Press night was 20 February 2002. The cast was as follows:

DAN	Guy Lankester
RONNIE	Ben Miles
CASS	Rebecca Egan
LOU	Tilly Blackwood
DOUGLAS	Simon Coates
HELEN	Sarah Alexander

Director Gemma Bodinetz
Designer Soutra Gilmour
Lighting Designer Tim Mitchell

Characters
DAN
RONNIE
CASS
LOU
DOUGLAS
HELEN

ACT ONE

The top of Parliament Hill, overlooking the City of London spreading into the distance.

Late afternoon in early summer, 1999. Two park benches. A lamp post.

A large, beaten up old holdall sits on a bench, wearing fresh travelling tags.

RONNIE *stands on the bench looking at the view. He wears loose, crumpled clothes for travelling rough, and sandals, also past their best. He slowly scans the horizon. After a while he places one hand over one eye, looks at the view, and then removes the hand. He looks at the view, and then replaces the hand over his eye. He looks at the view and removes the hand, as* DAN *approaches from the left and stops a little way away, watching this hand choreography.*

Pause.

DAN. Let me guess.

RONNIE (*without turning*). Money says you won't.

DAN. A very small animal just flew into your face. Probably not furry.

RONNIE. Make it *a lot* of money.

DAN. You just suffered a discrete stroke.

RONNIE. Not even close.

DAN. I give up.

RONNIE. You'll owe me a lot of money.

DAN. You know where I live – when I get a lot of money, it's yours.

RONNIE (*beat*). I'm trying to remember how the horizon was before I went away.

DAN. Don't waste your time. In a few months they'll put up the Millennium wheel and it'll all look completely different again.

RONNIE. I don't want it to all look completely different.

RONNIE *regards the view. Pause.*

The view from up here's still the best.

DAN. They say the view from the wheel's going to be even better.

RONNIE. If that's true it will only be because when you're on it, you won't actually be able to *see* it.

DAN. From what I've seen so far, I like it.

RONNIE *(turning to face* DAN *for the first time)*. 'Course you do, Dan. You kept hamsters.

RONNIE *gets off the bench and faces his old friend. Pause.* DAN *smiles.*

DAN. How was the flight?

RONNIE. You're looking at a man who got bumped up.

DAN. You got bumped up?

RONNIE. Club class.

DAN. No!

RONNIE. Oh yes!

DAN. Between lessons I sometimes stare out of the window at passing aeroplanes, and fantasise about paying economy but flying Club. What did you do?

RONNIE. What did I do?

DAN. You must've *done* something.

RONNIE. To what end?

DAN. To catch their eye. What was that eye-catching thing? Your trick?

RONNIE. No trick.

DAN. But I once read there's a knack for selection. For being singled out. To increase one's chances. What was yours?

RONNIE. During the flight I sat next to an erudite orthodox couple from Manhattan wearing matching velvet loafers. I thought they would be very dull, but they were completely the opposite. I think we had a very fascinating discussion over champagne as we crossed the Med.

DAN. You *think*?

RONNIE. My attention was distracted by how much better free food tastes when people in the next seat paid through both nostrils for theirs.

DAN. I thought you had to at least look smart to get bumped up. Did you look smarter before? Did you change in the plane? Or when you landed?

RONNIE. This is how I looked when I got bumped up.

DAN. I find that very difficult to swallow.

RONNIE. I swear.

DAN. It flies in the face of everything I respect.

RONNIE. I was standing in Ben Gurion waiting to check in, when a woman from the airline walked over, took my ticket, and handed me a better one.

DAN. Then you must've been standing differently. Show me how were you standing?

RONNIE. I wasn't standing differently.

DAN. You were standing like somebody special. Do it.

RONNIE. Do it?

DAN. Do how you were standing.

RONNIE. I stood like I'm standing now. Can you believe I slept like a rock over the Alps?

DAN. French or Swiss?

RONNIE. The plane flew between both.

DAN. You slept with Alps either side?

RONNIE. Full stretch. Pillow. Blanket. Eye patch. Ear plugs. Air socks. Little basket of petit fours.

DAN. Air socks?

RONNIE. In a sterilised polythene bag.

DAN. You slipped them on?

RONNIE. In Club Class it's *de rigueur*.

DAN. What were they like to fly in? Comfy? Snug?

RONNIE. From today I refuse to fly in anything else.

DAN. You always did land on your feet.

RONNIE. I'm taking it as an omen.

DAN. An omen?

RONNIE. For my return.

The two men look at one another. Pause.

DAN. Pinched myself when I heard your voice from Heathrow. Got other people to pinch me. You didn't give any hint you were coming home.

RONNIE. I only made up my mind a week ago. I would've come back immediately. But it's coming into the busy season, so I had to wait for a flight.

DAN. After so long, why the big hurry to leave?

RONNIE. Because there's nothing for me there, Dan.

DAN. What do you mean?

RONNIE. I mean . . . there's nothing for me there.

Pause. They regard one another.

DAN. I have an overwhelming urge to hug you.

RONNIE. It's been a long time.

RONNIE *opens his arms wide for embracing. Pause.*

DAN. What, you want me to come over there?

RONNIE. I'm flexible.

DAN. You're the one who's come home. You're the one who rang from the airport asking to meet before you've even spoken to your parents.

RONNIE. For a very good reason.

ACT ONE 11

DAN. Nevertheless.

RONNIE. You expressed the urge to hug, Dan.

DAN. I don't want to rush over like a dick. I'm feeling a torrent of emotion right now, which is fine because you're my oldest friend and I haven't seen you in four years. But I'm not going to fall at your feet like an idiot.

RONNIE regards DAN for a few moments.

RONNIE. Have you changed?

DAN. Well . . .

RONNIE. Put on a little weight, perhaps? Lost some hair?

DAN. Hair's not important.

RONNIE. But how we hug is?

DAN. I always used to be the second one. Ronnie and Danny. Starsky and Hutch – never Hutch and Starsky. Only I'm not a kid any more. I'm thirty five, with a kid of my own.

RONNIE. I know that.

DAN. I think it's important to state. If you're back for good, it's important to start as we mean to continue.

RONNIE. Okay.

DAN. I'm over the moon you're home, but it's important to recognise how things are.

RONNIE (*beat*). And I recognise that by coming over to you?

DAN. Better yet, would be moving towards one another simultaneously.

DAN opens his arms. RONNIE opens his. The two men face one another with their arms outstretched. Pause.

RONNIE. Who's going to make the first step?

DAN. I suggest a count of three.

DAN counts down with his fingers. They slowly walk towards one another and embrace affectionately. They hold each other tightly in silence for several moments.

God, it's good to see you . . .

RONNIE. You too, Dan. I can't tell you . . .

DAN. The twat who took your season ticket's a tosser.

RONNIE. Why I called from the airport –

DAN. Thinks he's at the Clock end – jumps on his seat when the game goes quiet and tries to get us all to chant. Doesn't understand that's why we sit where we're sitting.

RONNIE. Dan?

DAN. That we've passed through the 'leaping about and chanting like a tosser' phase, and are now in the 'sitting down and actually watching the game' phase.

RONNIE. Dan, I need a place to stay.

DAN. Tonight? Have the sofabed, no problem.

RONNIE. Not just tonight.

DAN. Not just tonight?

Beat.

Okay . . .

They break away. RONNIE *takes out a packet of cigarettes and lights one.* DAN *watches him.*

RONNIE (*casually*). You remember the night before I left?

DAN. Of course. We got hammered and urinated off the roof.

RONNIE. The night before I left, before we got hammered and urinated off the roof, you made me a promise. I didn't ask you to. It was a spontaneous gesture on your part.

DAN. If it's about keeping in regular touch you've always known I'm a lousy correspondent.

RONNIE. It wasn't a promise about keeping in regular touch, Dan.

DAN. Okay.

RONNIE. The night before I left you promised that my room in the flat would always be here for me.

DAN. Your room in the flat?

ACT ONE 13

RONNIE. Would always be here for me. That was your promise. That was what you promised me. *Unsolicited.*

DAN. That was a long time ago. And made – if not entirely under the influence – pretty close to it.

RONNIE. As you say, a long time ago. Four years, one month, and twenty-six days.

DAN. During which time I've been married and divorced.

RONNIE. I know.

DAN. Become a father.

RONNIE. If you're worried about rent –

DAN. Rent doesn't come into it.

RONNIE. I'll put an envelope on the kitchen table at the end of each month. Or if you'd prefer, we could set up something more formal.

DAN. It's not a question of *letting* the room.

RONNIE. If it's because you're seeing Cass, I give you my word. I'll be less than a fly on the wall.

DAN. You don't understand.

RONNIE. Believe me, the last thing I'd want is to be present when the two of you . . . My oldest friend and my sister? No offence, but just thinking of the two of you locked together turns my stomach.

DAN (*beat*). It's my boy's room now.

RONNIE. Your boy's room?

DAN. It's Oscar's room now.

RONNIE (*beat*). But you told me he lives with your ex. I distinctly remember reading an email –

DAN. And when he comes to stay, he stays in his room.

RONNIE. You mean my room.

DAN. Now it's his. Gunners curtains. Denis Bergkamp duvet. Ray Parlour pillowcase. I sleep there myself sometimes, when the weather ... sometimes in a storm. Or if my day has been particularly shit.

RONNIE. May I refer you back to your promise ...

DAN. Made in a universe without Oscar.

RONNIE. Move Oscar into the studio.

Pause.

DAN. Why won't you –

RONNIE. You haven't made a film in years. Gut your studio and move Oscar's stuff in there. He's three years old, Dan. He won't even notice.

DAN (*beat*). Gut my studio?

RONNIE. Do you good. Scorched earth, with nothing left to torture yourself over what might have been.

DAN. I'm not tortured over what might have been.

RONNIE. Nevertheless, problems solved all round.

DAN (*beat*). Okay.

Beat.

Look.

Beat.

Right.

Beat.

Even if I did that.

RONNIE. If you did, it would be the right thing to do – believe me.

DAN. Even if I *did* move Oscar into the studio.

RONNIE. Which, for the purposes of this conversation, I feel we should now call 'Oscar's cosy new bedroom'.

DAN. Even if I moved him across, you can't come back.

RONNIE. But my point, Dan, is that I could. More to the point, I sort of came home on the back of that promise.

DAN. But you should have checked first. Surely you understand this.

RONNIE. I just assumed you'd keep your word.

DAN (*starting to lose his patience for the first time*). I'm sorry, Ronnie. But I need the flat clear.

RONNIE. Need?

Beat.

DAN. For me and Cass.

RONNIE. Like I *said*, when she's round –

DAN. But my hope is that in the not-too-distant future Cass will *always* be round.

Pause.

RONNIE. I didn't realise things had become that serious.

DAN. I know what you're thinking.

RONNIE. I'm not thinking anything.

DAN. You're thinking, 'oh the irony'.

RONNIE. I wasn't thinking 'oh the irony,' Dan.

DAN. How could a misdirected email from you cause your best friend and your sister to get together?

RONNIE. I wasn't thinking that.

DAN. Well, we got together, Ron. More to the point, I'm entertaining the serious hope that we're going to stay together.

RONNIE *takes out his packet of cigarettes and lights another.*

I see you smoke now.

RONNIE (*more insistent*). You made a promise, Dan. I don't want to put you on the spot. But a promise is a promise or else *it's* a lie, and *you're* a liar.

DAN. Like I said a few minutes ago –

RONNIE (*more insistent*). If a promise is to have *any* value it has to override temporary changes in circumstances. The country I've just flown from would never have got off the ground if some rather extraordinary people hadn't held fast to a two- thousand-year-old covenant – it's what sustained them until willpower and tragedy forced Israel onto the map. It's what's sustaining some of them *still* – even as they're told on a daily basis that the doctrine of all or nothing is unacceptable.

DAN. Hang on –

RONNIE. A *true* promise between people who mean what they say is a powerful thing, Dan. It's simplicity is its strength.

DAN. Jesus, Ron. When did you get this emphatic?

RONNIE. If we remain unchanged by travel why leave the comfort of the sofa?

DAN. Ask me for anything else.

RONNIE. I don't *need* anything else. It's either the flat or back to my parents.

DAN. So go back to your parents.

RONNIE. I can't.

DAN. Why not?

RONNIE. I'm thirty-six years old.

DAN. You always used to say that in their eyes you never stopped being twelve.

RONNIE. Exactly.

He takes a deep drag and then drops the cigarette on the floor – crushing it underfoot.

So I'm going to ask you one more time.

DAN. Four years ago I would have ummed and aahed and given in. But not now. I no longer um and aah and I'm not giving in. I'm sorry.

RONNIE. I don't wanna have to beg.

DAN. I'd do anything for you. You know that.

RONNIE. So I can come back to the flat?

RONNIE picks up his holdall and slings it over his shoulder.

DAN. Anything but that.

They regard one another for several moments, before DAN exits stage right.

RONNIE slowly sits on the bench facing front, sharp daylight blending into dusk over the city. He pulls his jacket close around him, turning up the collar against the cool evening air. He looks straight ahead, smoking the cigarette, watched by CASS, who has appeared stage left.

CASS. That's new.

RONNIE (*standing*). If we only ever did what we've only ever done we'd still be squatting in caves, wiping our arses with moss.

RONNIE stubs out the cigarette on the arm of the bench, and stands.

You look very well.

CASS crosses into the scene proper.

CASS. You mean *older*.

RONNIE. Older doesn't suit everyone. You it suits.

CASS. You've started to go grey.

RONNIE. In Israel, grey is the new light black this season.

They smile and embrace.

CASS. You sounded a little tense on the 'phone. How is it at mum and dad's?

They pull apart.

RONNIE. You have to ask?

CASS. I meant . . . how *bad*?

RONNIE (*sitting*). Well . . . I'm tending not to get up until I hear dad leave for work. And mum's been slipping me a fiver for dinner before he gets back. I'll either sit in a burger bar ingesting the carcinogenic fog of vaporised animal fat, or come up here 'til it's past his bedtime.

CASS. It's only been a few days, Ronnie. Give him time.

RONNIE. Time? Yesterday I made the mistake of going home too early. I heard him through their bedroom door telling mum he wished either he or I was dead.

CASS. You must've expected a certain level of disappointment. They put a lot of eggs in you.

RONNIE. Well . . . all smashed now as far as they're concerned.

CASS. Don't be so melodramatic.

RONNIE. Our father wishes I was *dead*, Cass – I think we've inched ever so slightly beyond melodrama, don't you?

CASS. There was a time when dad's penchant for talking like a character out of Sophocles had you in stitches.

RONNIE. This time there was no playing to the gallery. This time he meant it.

CASS. I'm sure you think –

RONNIE (*adamant*). This time he meant it.

Pause. CASS *regards her brother as he takes out the packet of cigarettes to light another, and takes a deep drag.*

CASS. What happened with the doctorate?

RONNIE. It wasn't for me.

CASS (*taking a deep breath*). Why didn't you tell me you'd dropped out over a year ago? Do you know what it felt like to find out yesterday?

RONNIE. When I told dad he told me not to tell you, in case mum found out.

CASS. Good old fashioned Jewish patriarchy – don't you just love it? So between dropping out and coming home you did *what* out there?

RONNIE. A lot of things.

CASS. Such as?

RONNIE. All sorts.

CASS. Anything specific you're bursting to elaborate about?

RONNIE. Not really.

CASS. Okay. So why come home now? Run out of money?

RONNIE. No.

CASS. Luck?

RONNIE. No.

CASS. Arrested? Thrown out for doing a Vanunu? Your emails dried up ages ago – give me some kind of clue. Did you just get bored?

RONNIE. Anyone who can get bored in Israel is clinically dead.

CASS. So why?

RONNIE. The situation became impossible.

CASS. The situation? But everyone's saying Barak's going to be better than Netanyahu. Best chance of a breakthrough in years, I read.

RONNIE. Look – can't we just leave it that I couldn't stay.

CASS. Jesus, Ronnie, but *why* couldn't you?!

RONNIE (*standing*). Let me ask you a question.

CASS. No, but hang on –

RONNIE (*turning on her*). Dan.

CASS. Dan?

RONNIE. Dan.

CASS. What about Dan?

RONNIE. You like him?

CASS. Obviously.

RONNIE. Love?

CASS. While you were away I discovered there's considerably more to Daniel than meets the eye. I've developed the view that you were a bad influence.

RONNIE. Oh really. Well, I could tell *you* some salty stories about Danny.

CASS. No need. He already told me the really disgusting ones.

RONNIE. And you still like him?

CASS. You know how much of a sucker I am for reformed bad lads.

RONNIE. And Malcolm and Josie?

CASS. Malcolm and Josie?

RONNIE. They like Dan?

CASS. You've been taking him to their house for years. You know they've always liked him.

RONNIE. When he was with me he wasn't a horny Gentile *schtupping* one of their children.

CASS. When we've been round on Friday night I don't think mum and dad were gazing into their soup picturing Dan doing me over the table. I may be wrong. Oh shit . . .

RONNIE. What?

CASS. That's what I'm going to be thinking Malcolm and Josie are thinking every time we go round. That won't erase. Great present on your return, though a face-pack from En Gedi would've been sufficient.

RONNIE. But the Jewish thing?

CASS. What Jewish thing?

RONNIE. I just wouldn't want you thinking something's not a problem when it possibly is.

CASS. What?

RONNIE. A problem.

CASS. The Jewish thing?

RONNIE. The Jewish thing.

CASS. Yes, but what are you actually talking about?

RONNIE. Surely it's better to be wide-eyed than blind to the possibility.

CASS. If I knew what possibility you're referring to I'd be better placed to agree.

RONNIE. I'm not saying I'm insensitive to the anxieties surrounding the issue.

CASS. Which issue?

RONNIE. I'm simply saying let's not pretend they don't exist.

CASS. Mum and dad and Dan?

RONNIE. I'm only saying.

CASS. Well you don't have to. Because even if there was a problem, which there isn't. But even if there was, Dan took care of it.

RONNIE. He took care of it?

CASS. Dan's Arsenal. Dad's Tottenham. Dan plays *goy* to Dad's *yid*. Since we started seeing one another Dan's used the difference as their common ground.

RONNIE. Dan did that?

CASS. Perky banter about who's higher than who in the table. I don't know what the Hell they're talking about but they get on fine.

RONNIE. And that works with mum?

CASS. She asks as subtle as a sledgehammer if we've 'talked about the future'. I tell her our generation finds it difficult to even *think* about the future let alone talk about it. But with my track record, she's so relieved I'm with someone who changes his pants and doesn't dribble, she won't push it.

RONNIE. And you?

CASS. What do you mean?

RONNIE. We both know how deep it goes, even if we don't think it does.

CASS. You're not suggesting *I* have a problem with Dan not being Jewish?

RONNIE. I don't think you *think* you have. But if you had it would hardly be a failure on your part.

CASS. Are you serious?

RONNIE. It wouldn't be seen as some lapse in decency. It's what's been done to you. How you've been indoctrinated.

CASS. *Indoctrinated*?

RONNIE. Indoctrination. Heritage. Call it what you will. Either way it's beyond your control.

CASS (*bridling at the suggestion*). Have I *ever* expressed a problem with Dan not being Jewish before?

RONNIE. You weren't going out with him before.

CASS. I'm finding it difficult to believe I'm actually hearing this.

RONNIE. I ask only because on the day I came back I came straight from the airport and met him up here.

CASS. I know.

RONNIE. I asked if I could move back –

CASS. – into the flat. Yes, Ronnie. I know.

RONNIE. And he said I couldn't, because he was keeping the flat clear.

CASS. For Oscar. I *know*. Contrary to what you might wish to believe, your best friend and I enjoy a pretty full-blown relationship – with all the open lines of communication that entails.

RONNIE. Except Dan isn't just keeping the flat clear for Oscar, is he?

CASS (*beat*). What do you mean, not just for Oscar?

RONNIE. You haven't discussed moving in together?

ACT ONE 23

CASS (*beat*). What?

RONNIE. You've not even *considered* the possibility?

CASS. Wait a second –

RONNIE. You see, this is what I find interesting. Because Dan *has*.

CASS *stares at* RONNIE, *wrong-footed.* DAN *strolls up the hill and onto the scene holding a remote-controlled car control unit* (*box with an aerial coming out of the top*) *and looking back in the direction from which he's just come.*

DAN. Has it run out already?!

RONNIE *leans forward and gently kisses the top of his sister's head, before walking away.*

CASS *looks up and watches him go as* DAN *fiddles with the controls.*

I've been using it for all of what – ten minutes? How can I give him this?

CASS. Be honest. It was never really a present for Oscar anyway.

DAN. Of course it was.

CASS. How many three-year-olds do you see with remote control cars?

DAN (*walking off to collect the car*). Perhaps the batteries hold up better on flat ground.

CASS *watches as* DAN *returns holding a shiny plastic, fairly cheap-looking remote-controlled car.*

This was going to be a major part of my attempt to get him outdoors. His mother's big on videos, but since when was *watching* the same as *doing*? No-one's saying she's a bad mother. Just a lazy one.

CASS. A little rich considering you don't have him full-time.

DAN. Just because my contact can't be full time needn't mean my concern isn't.

CASS. Come here.

DAN (*crossing to* CASS). What?

CASS (*pulling him closer by his lapels*). I know how your mind works, Dan.

DAN. You couldn't possibly. I'm an enigma.

CASS. As a child you always hankered after a radio-controlled car, but your parents never had the excess wherewithal to waste on anything so pointless. But now *you* have, you're at an age where prowling round your local rec in dim, solitary pursuit of a miniaturised vehicle would be a sad comment on you and your kind. So you buy the toy under the guise of buying it for your three-year-old – a little boy, lest we forget, with insufficient strength in his arms to snap a wet match, let alone wield a radio control unit.

DAN (*smiling. Beat*). I was going to whip up a leather harness.

CASS. A leather harness?

DAN. Toddler *Leiderhosen*, with attachments.

CASS. Toddler *Leiderhosen*?

DAN. With any leftover leather I was planning to knock you up a pair.

CASS. Oh really.

DAN. Slim-fitting. Cut high on the –

CASS *puts a finger on his mouth, stopping him. They regard one another for a few moments*

(*With* CASS*'s finger still on his mouth.*) I lub do.

CASS. Don't say that.

DAN (*removing her finger*). But I do.

CASS. Say it after I've been jogging and I've got a roast potato face and a sweaty arse.

DAN *adjusts himself.*

What?

DAN. You're bending my antenna.

CASS. Dan, I need to talk to you.

DAN. You are talking to me.

CASS. Seriously.

DAN. That sounds serious.

CASS. About us.

DAN. Should I sit down?

CASS. Are your legs tired?

> CASS *moves off a little and turns to face* DAN, *holding the car.*
>
> Ronnie told me not to tell you, but I get the impression he hasn't grasped the shift in loyalties since you and I started seeing each other.

DAN. Ronnie told you not to tell me what?

CASS. That he told me something you told him.

DAN. I didn't tell him anything.

CASS. About us.

DAN. Us?

Pause.

CASS. That you hoped I'd move in with you one day.

DAN (*beat*). I see.

CASS. And I just wanted to make something absolutely clear.

DAN. Is the hope unfounded?

CASS. I just wanted to make it absolutely clear that the reason I've never voiced a similar hope has nothing to do with the fact that you're not Jewish.

DAN. What?

CASS. In case you were thinking it might have.

DAN. It never occurred to me.

CASS. No?

DAN. Not for a single, solitary second.

They regard one another, as LOU *pushes a pram to the top of the hill and takes a breather.*

Long pause.

CASS *gets up from the bench and moves away, looking out over the view.*

LOU. A single, solitary second?

CASS (*still looking at* DAN). That's what he said.

LOU. And this is a problem because?

CASS (*still looking at* DAN). Because when I thought about it . . . I thought perhaps he should have.

LOU. Uhuh.

CASS. I mean, if he's as serious about me as he so often professes it's an issue he should at least be alive to. If not from his own point of view, then from mine.

DAN *crosses to* CASS *and kisses her.*

DAN (*tenderly*). Love you, Cassie.

He walks out of the scene.

LOU. Isn't it enough to hold people accountable for the things they *do* think?

CASS. It just flagged another little question, that's all.

LOU. Another little question? Or yet another little question *mark*?

CASS. You don't think it's a legitimate concern?

LOU. Is Daniel a long-term prospect, yes or no? You want to come to a conclusion you won't regret, of *course* I can understand that.

CASS. But your problem is?

LOU. My problem is less with your need to come to the right conclusion, than the agonising you're going through to reach it.

CASS. I've been burned too many times.

LOU. You've a predilection for arseholes, free-loaders, and man-boys. You're hardly alone.

CASS. My emotional skin is a veritable lattice of shiny scars on shiny scars.

LOU. It's not helped by the fact that it's getting easier and easier for a bit of old chaff to pass himself off as wheat. You have to fan hard to expose the dross. *But* –

CASS. If I fanned any harder I'd take off.

LOU. But fan *too* hard and you could be left with nothing. Just you, in a field, empty-handed.

CASS (*not sure what* LOU *actually thinks*). So . . . you *don't* think I should be concerned by Dan not being concerned about the Jewish thing?

LOU. What I think is . . . what do *you* think?

CASS. My brother suggested I'm reluctant to admit an innate aversion to the idea of a permanent relationship with a non-Jew.

LOU. The question is, is he right?

CASS. The question is, if he *is* right, what does that make me?

LOU. A traditionalist.

CASS. Or some kind of a racist?

LOU. Well, that all depends how you look at it.

CASS. I'm doing my best to look at it as honestly as possible. I don't know, Lou. The greatest bigot I ever knew? Guess.

LOU. In real life?

CASS. My grandmother.

LOU. On whose side?

CASS. Mum's. One minute she was a lovely old woman in pressure stockings, shouting at minor celebrities on TV to get their hair cut. And next she was a wrinkled ball of malevolence, screeching venom at Blacks, Asians, Catholics – you name it, and if it wasn't Jewish she hated it.

LOU. Jesus.

CASS. I can't help but wonder if a little bit of that managed to wheedle its way onto my chromosomes.

LOU. You haven't got a bigoted bone in your body.

CASS. Not that I know of. We like to think that our past means we've cornered the market in racial tolerance. But Nana alone kicks that little bit of self-aggrandizement into touch.

LOU. Maybe, but nothing wrong with sticking to your own kind in principle.

CASS. You didn't.

LOU. I said there's nothing wrong with it. I didn't say you had to turn it into a fetish. Anyway, Doug's vague Methodism hardly posed the greatest hurdle for a Catholic in guilt and reverence for ceremony only.

CASS. I've gone out with non-Jewish guys before. I've certainly slept with them. Lots of them. Very nice they were too.

LOU. You've slept with them, but have you ever thought about moving in with any of them?

CASS. I've come close.

LOU. You've come close but never completed. What does that tell you?

CASS. That I'm a sexually predatory hypocrite?

LOU. It's a possibility. But only one of several.

CASS. Yet taken as a whole, Lou. My unease about Dan being married when we started seeing each other. My concerns about becoming a fixture in his son's life, and the trauma that could result from a break-up. The Jew non-Jew thing, and the revelation that he's not given it a single solitary second of thought. And don't forget, these are all in addition to the litany of more general anxieties – such as my chances of finding someone else *as good* if not better. Compatibility. Reliability. How we raise any children we might have? To circumcise or not in the event we had a boy? The possible friction arising from the fact that I earn twice as much as Dan. Dan's capacity for violence, mental or physical.

LOU. Physical? You mean, Dan –

CASS. No of course not. But I've noticed if we ever watch a documentary about the African savannah, he always roots for the cheetah, never the gazelle.

LOU (*beat*). Right . . .

CASS. And then there are my parents to consider.

LOU. Malcolm and Josie?

CASS. Though I've never said as much to Dan, I've consciously been keeping our relationship uncomplicated in their eyes.

LOU. How uncomplicated?

CASS. Very much on a day-to-day basis, with little or no emphasis on what may or may not develop.

LOU. I see.

CASS. In many ways it was so much easier for them. I don't mean economically, but their choices were so much more straightforward for being limited. On a simple geographical level, my parents rarely mixed socially beyond their Jewish circle, so the chances of going out with a non-Jew – let alone marrying one – were so much slighter.

LOU. But you're not talking about marrying, Dan.

CASS. I'm only talking about the possibility of *moving in* with him. But the resonance is never far away. As are the overriding fears, which are perhaps more real to them than they seem to me.

LOU. The overriding fears?

CASS. For the gradual disintegration of the community.

LOU. Never a fear with us Catholics – abstract or concrete.

CASS. And yet.

LOU. And yet?

DOUGLAS, LOU*'s husband, comes up the path from the left, holding a serious-looking stunt kite and re-winding the twine back on its spool. He stops within hearing range of* CASS *and* LOU, *though they don't see him. He listens as he spools the twine.*

CASS. And yet, whether I set out to or not, I seem to have fallen for Danny boy. So taken as a whole –

LOU. Is it possible to take all this as a whole?

CASS. Taken as a whole, what do you think I should do?

LOU (*beat*). No, Cass. Don't do that.

CASS. Don't do what?

LOU. Don't lead yourself up the garden path and then ask me to knock on the door for you.

CASS. Is that what I was doing?

LOU. Your brother's really stirred your porridge, hasn't he.

DOUGLAS (*advancing a few steps and pointing into the distance*). You see that couple beside that tree under that blanket . . .

CASS *and* LOU *look over.*

CASS. There ought to be a law.

DOUGLAS. Or failing a law, a mounted short-range telescope for interested voyeurs.

LOU (*hinting broadly*). Douglas. Why don't you carry on flying your kite. You know. Somewhere else.

DOUGLAS. You may not have noticed, but what wind there was has dropped like a stone.

LOU. Only, Cass and I were talking.

DOUGLAS. Oh? About anything interesting?

LOU. I doubt to you.

CASS. My brother thinks I might be an unconscious religious fanatic with a fascistic libido.

LOU. He's somehow managed to plant the idea that the reason Cass hasn't been *actively* thinking about Dan in the long-term might be rooted in their religious differences.

DOUGLAS. I didn't think you were religious, Cass.

CASS. I'm not.

DOUGLAS. I didn't think Dan was either.

CASS. He isn't.

DOUGLAS. I'm so relieved you cleared that up.

CASS. It's easy for you. You don't really believe in anything.

DOUGLAS. Not easy at all. It takes a lot of effort not to believe in anything.

LOU. And anyway that's not true. He does.

DOUGLAS. No I don't.

LOU. Equality, justice, freedom with opportunity. All that stuff.

DOUGLAS. Oh, all that stuff's a given. You have to understand how all that stuff works, but it's too obviously right to require concerted *belief.*

LOU. It's what makes him the only ideological taxman in the Inland Revenue.

DOUGLAS. Well, you want the good life, pay for it.

LOU. Yes, Doug. We know.

DOUGLAS. Don't want to pay taxes? Fine. Buy yourself a large gun, turn out the lights, and wait for them to come for what's yours.

LOU. Please, Doug.

DOUGLAS. Doesn't take a genius. Everything has a price. Only question worth asking: are you prepared to pay for what you want, or not?

LOU. He's only telling you all this because I stopped listening years ago.

CASS (*sotto*). I'm not really listening. Just giving the appearance.

LOU. I find occasional little grunts convey interest where none exists.

DOUGLAS. And there was I hoping the feminist struggle amounted to a little more than taking the piss.

LOU. Also, tilting your head to one side in mock fascination.

CASS. A simple question often keeps Dan chauntering on indefinitely, without requiring any response this side of actually falling asleep.

DOUGLAS has been re-winding the twine on the kite as the two women talk.

DOUGLAS. What Lou and I have *really* been wondering about you and Dan, Cass . . .

LOU and CASS suddenly turn to DOUGLAS. Beat.

Oh. Listening?

LOU (*trying to head him off at the pass*). Doug.

CASS. No. Go on.

DOUGLAS. Why he hasn't asked you to move in with him before now?

LOU. Now is neither the time –

CASS. No, Doug's a friend. I'd be interested in a male perspective.

LOU. Then Douglas isn't your man.

DOUGLAS (*ignoring his wife*). Dan's been married before, so he's obviously not opposed to cohabitation in one form or another.

LOU. Did it ever occur to you that he's perhaps once bitten twice shy.

DOUGLAS. It's a nice expression but hardly holds up. It's the equivalent of flipping a coin, getting tails, and then believing you've got more or less chance of getting heads with the next flip. Surely, regardless what happened before, either Cass is or isn't the woman for him now.

CASS. He has been *thinking* about asking me to move in.

DOUGLAS. Unfortunately, the fact that he's been thinking about it without discussing it – that he's only come clean because your brother blew the gaff. Well. I'm sorry, Cass. But speaking as a *male* and a *friend*, it almost makes the situation worse.

LOU (*to* CASS). Excuse us for a moment.

LOU *takes* DOUGLAS *by the elbow and leads him firmly away from* CASS.

DOUGLAS. I know what you're going to say.

LOU. The question of why Dan hasn't yet asked Cass to move in arose as part of a private conversation between *us*.

DOUGLAS. Rather than you and I gossiping among ourselves about what Dan may or may not be thinking, I thought it might be more pertinent to ask – if not the horse's mouth – then at least the person who kisses it.

LOU. You have no idea what's happening inside her head right now.

DOUGLAS. It's always been my understanding that complicated issues become progressively *less* complicated when you actually talk about them – the key syllables in that sentence being *pro* and *gress*.

LOU. You really don't understand what's going on here, so I would greatly appreciate it if you would, please, not speak.

LOU *turns to walk back to* CASS, *but* DOUGLAS *grabs her arm and pulls her back.*

DOUGLAS. Whenever you tell me 'I don't understand' all you mean is I don't happen to agree with you. As though disagreement in itself is a form of betrayal. It's a cheap way of silencing an opposing view, but if that's ultimately your aim it would at least be more honest if you simply punched me in the mouth.

LOU. Don't tempt me.

DOUGLAS. Take your best shot.

LOU (*on the attack*). Dan is a lovely, lovely man!

DOUGLAS (*matching her*). Who doesn't know what he wants!

LOU. That's not true! He seems to be wanting to live with Cass.

DOUGLAS. *Seems* to be. At some point in the near or distant future. For some period of time, hitherto unspecified. I'm very fond of Cass – I don't want to see her hurt any more than you do!

CASS. Um. You do know I can hear you.

LOU *and* DOUGLAS *freeze. Pause.*

I didn't think it was fair to let you carry on thinking I couldn't.

LOU. You heard what we've just been saying?

CASS. I just don't think you're very good at being discrete.

LOU. I think we must be out of practise around grown-ups. Around Claire we don't need to be anymore discrete than we would if we were talking in front of a small cat, or a log.

CASS (*to* DOUGLAS). Do you really think Dan might not actually know what he wants?

LOU. Don't ask him, he doesn't even know how to park straight.

DOUGLAS. Untrue. I just choose not to.

LOU (*to* DOUGLAS). Why don't you take chummy back to the car? The sun's gone in.

DOUGLAS. She's wrapped up like an immersion heater.

LOU (*firmly*). Douglas, it wasn't a request.

LOU *regards* DOUGLAS *firmly. Beat.*

DOUGLAS (*taking a deep breath, repeating as rote*). Why don't I take chummy back to the car. It's getting cold.

DOUGLAS *crosses to* CASS *and kisses her on the cheek.*

Listen to Lou, Cass. I mean it. Everything will be fine. You're lovely. Dan's lovely. We're all lovely, lovely people in a lovely, lovely world.

DOUGLAS *peers for a moment into the pram and then wheels it back down the hill.* LOU *and* CASS *watch him go.*

LOU. Dan's what, thirty-four?

CASS. Thirty-five.

LOU. His failed marriage aside, would it be any wonder if he was proceeding with due caution?

CASS. Douglas didn't say 'due caution'. Douglas said 'uncertainty'.

LOU. Isn't it around their mid thirties that men of Dan's age face the realisation that they're never going to slide the winner past Brazil in the world cup final? Row the Atlantic. Or in Dan's case, win the best original short category at the Sundance Film Festival.

CASS. I think Dan came to terms with that one a while ago.

LOU. But don't we see them on the tube every morning? Showered, bleary-eyed, wondering how in God's name they ended up with a silk noose round their neck, comedy socks, a low sperm count, and an annually renewable travelcard.

CASS. If we have to be realistically aware of the clock why can't they?

LOU. I'm merely suggesting that Dan's prudence might be all the more authentic for being measured.

CASS. We started exchanging emails three-and-a-half years into his failing marriage, and when that broke up we started seeing each other. From her to me. Before her, someone else, and before someone else, if you examine the chronology, someone else again. I saw it all from the vantage point of Ronnie's sister, don't forget. Turns out, when you put all Dan's dates together, there's scarcely three months between one woman and the next.

LOU. Not wanting to be lonely is hardly a crime, Cass.

CASS. But if he's really not sure about me, how sure can I be about him?

LOU *regards her friend for a few moments.*

LOU. Please don't do this.

CASS. Don't do what?

LOU. Don't talk yourself out of being happy.

LOU sets off after DOUGLAS, leaving CASS standing alone for a few moments.

Pause.

The light darkens to late night, the bench illuminated by a pool of orange sodium. City lights sparkle in the distance.

CASS pulls her coat around her and turns the collar up. She looks at her watch impatiently.

After a few moments RONNIE slowly walks onto the scene behind her, holding a white plastic carrier bag. He silently lowers the bag to the floor and stealthily advances on CASS from behind, grabbing her, and putting his hand over her mouth.

RONNIE. One sound and I'll slit your throat . . .

CASS's eyes widen in terror, but she instinctively raises her arm and drives her elbow hard into RONNIE's side.

Fuck!

RONNIE immediately releases his sister who turns round and sees who it is.

CASS. You stupid fucking cunt! Do you know precisely *how* unfunny that was?!

RONNIE sinks to his knees in agony. He is unable to speak, just moans, quietly.

We're not kids anymore, you *prick*!

RONNIE (*severely winded*). It was meant to be a joke . . .

CASS (*the anger focusing*). You were *meant* to be here three quarters of an hour ago! Where the fuck have you been?!

RONNIE (*vaguely pointing in the direction of the carrier bag on the floor, still winded*). Felafel van by the Royal Free . . .

CASS (*furious*). Do you know how many invitations to *rape* I've had to decline while you were stuffing your face?!

RONNIE (*winded*). I was hungry.

CASS (*beat*). You were *what?*

Pause.

RONNIE (*low, winded*). Sorry.

CASS. Too fucking late.

RONNIE (*beat, winded*). Need to . . . sit.

RONNIE *offers his hand so* CASS *can help him to his feet. She doesn't move.*

CASS (*ignoring him*). The bench is over there.

CASS *doesn't move to help him – just watches* RONNIE *struggle to the bench. He sits, and breathes in a controlled rhythm. Pause. Finally he sits up, and lets out a deep breath.*

(*The anger subsiding, but leaving her feeling assertive.*) Mum says you're now avoiding all meals at home.

RONNIE. It's easier.

CASS. So why don't you leave altogether?

RONNIE. With what? To where?

CASS. I could lend you some rent-money until you got a job.

RONNIE. A job?

CASS. What tedious little people like me do.

RONNIE. I'm qualified to sit in academic libraries and read. Hardly puts me in a prime spot in the marketplace.

CASS. What about dad?

RONNIE. What about him?

CASS. Maybe there's something around the office you could do?

RONNIE. Be serious.

CASS. I am being serious.

RONNIE. What happened the last time I worked for him?

CASS. He gave you the sack after twenty-five minutes. But that was different. Now you know not to get his seventy-eight year old cutter mashed on cannabis. Though, she's not seventy-eight anymore, of course. She's dead. Nevertheless –

RONNIE. Anyway. I can't leave the house. Not yet.

CASS. Decide to leave and then leave. The rest takes care of itself.

RONNIE. Staying at mum and dad's isn't about not having to pay rent, Cass.

CASS. No – it's about being thirty-six and still not taking responsibility for yourself.

RONNIE. Oh please . . .

CASS. Oh please *nothing* – that's what it is.

RONNIE. You don't believe things could actually be ever so slightly more complex?

CASS. Israel was a flop, you can sniff forty on the breeze, with no clue where next to turn. No, I'm sorry, I really don't think it is any more complex than that.

RONNIE. *Think* about it –

CASS. Here we go.

RONNIE. Not 'here we go'. I came back with nothing. All that money, for what? He won't even talk to me.

CASS. Maybe it's gonna take him longer to cool down than you originally thought.

RONNIE. And maybe he never will. You know what he's like with a *broigus*.* He's got twenty-year-old feuds with cousins whose name he can no longer remember. And others he rings just to slam the 'phone down when they pick up. Am I exaggerating?

CASS. So he lives in black and white.

RONNIE. So if I walk away with the situation unresolved dad and I are probably finished. *Finished*, Cass. No-show at his

---

* *broigus* – quarrel, feud.

funeral. *Over*. Which has – if you only care to look – profound repercussions for everyone. Because if dad and I stop talking, mum and I stop talking – at least, until he dies.

CASS. I didn't ask you up here to listen to this.

RONNIE (*continuing his theory*). After he's dead – assuming he goes first – whatever feeling mum has left for me will be crippled by loyalty to his memory. Until she goes herself, angry and bitter.

CASS. If this is the sort of stuff you're thinking over there, the sooner you get out the better.

RONNIE (*concluding*). Inevitably you'll be drawn in and made to take sides. Which you'll refuse to do, or will be unable to resist – either way expanding the rifts already there in one direction or another – until it all caves in.

Beat.

For everyone's sake, I can't leave yet.

CASS *regards him. Pause.*

CASS. Did you know mum thinks you've been brainwashed?

RONNIE. In Israel . . . ?

CASS. She's no other way to account for something you said in response to an enquiry about whether you'd come across any nice Jewish girls.

RONNIE. Oh that. I merely said some of them would've seemed a lot nicer if they weren't so vitriolic about their Arab counterparts.

CASS. Perhaps they had a lot to be vitriolic about.

RONNIE. You have to hear some of the things that get said to believe them. Ordinary, decent people, spouting extraordinarily vile garbage.

CASS. Look, I'm not trying to defend people I've never met, in a situation I know relatively little about –

RONNIE. Good.

CASS. – I'm just trying to relate how worried mum is about you since you got back.

RONNIE. Mum goes to sleep worrying about the sunrise. If they severed her head from her neck she'd worry which bit most needed her scarf.

CASS. She rang me at work this morning.

RONNIE. So she's got your work number.

CASS. She told me they don't see the same Ronnie they drove to the airport four-and-a-half years ago.

RONNIE. It would be an indictment of foreign travel if they did.

CASS. But her implication was you're not *any* kind of Ronnie they can relate to.

RONNIE. Then what kind of Ronnie am I?

CASS. That's the problem. They don't *know*.

RONNIE. What do *you* think?

CASS. I can't say.

RONNIE. Look at me.

CASS. I'm looking.

RONNIE. Who am I?

CASS. You're Ronnie Stoll.

RONNIE. To *you*. Who am I to you?

CASS. You're my brother.

RONNIE. Looking at me, does that feel strange to say in any way?

CASS (*beat*). No.

RONNIE. You hesitated.

CASS. There's a different quality about your eyes.

RONNIE. In what way?

CASS. More sombre than I remember.

RONNIE. Yeah, well. It's dark.

RONNIE *stands and walks a little way away. He takes out a pack of cigarettes and lights one. He takes a deep drag.*

CASS (*watching*). Can I ask something?

RONNIE. I could never stop you in the past.

CASS. I've always wondered what effect living off mum and dad for most of your adult life must have had on you?

Beat.

RONNIE. You think I'm some kind of *leech*?

CASS. I imagined it couldn't be entirely healthy, that's all.

RONNIE. Cass, let's get one thing straight. I never took anything they didn't insist I take.

CASS. I wasn't implying –

RONNIE. Every penny was linked in one way or another to education. You know dad.

CASS. You're not listening to what I'm saying.

RONNIE. If you hit him for a few hundred for an old banger he'd ask 'there's something wrong with the bus?'

CASS. Ronnie –

RONNIE. But go to him for a few thousand for a Masters – his hand was a fucking blur he couldn't write a cheque fast enough.

CASS. The way you say that makes it sound like a bad thing.

RONNIE. Beyond a point there was a certain recklessness to it, certainly. I grew to regard them like a pair of speculators blindly pumping money into a potentially hot – yet ultimately flawed – proposition.

CASS. I wish they'd been a little more reckless with their chequebook towards me over the years.

RONNIE. For as long as I can remember I was cultivated to be the family brain.

CASS. You make it sound like we lived in the Hammer House of Horror.

RONNIE. You know what I mean. The scholarship boy. The school-prize winner. It was an image of me they were only too keen to sustain. All that reflected glory they could bask in. All that *naches*.* I'm not blaming them.

CASS. Maybe not right at this very moment – but I think I can hear the gears of blame *cranking* up.

RONNIE. I know it sounds like blame, but it isn't. It's just that somewhere along the road I ceased to be a sound investment. Trouble is, they never stopped investing. I thought perhaps they couldn't. Like inveterate gamblers putting their shirt on one last punt after another in the hope that one would come good. Over the last couple of years I've realised it was much more desperate than that.

CASS. What're you talking about?

RONNIE. I'll give an illustration. Just over a year ago, when I contacted dad to let him know my PhD had collapsed, I assumed my subsidy would stop immediately, with an instruction to return home forthwith.

CASS. It didn't?

RONNIE. The call to come back never came. And in fact the subsidy *increased*.

CASS. Increased?

RONNIE. Think about what that signals.

CASS. I don't understand.

RONNIE. It signalled that as long as I remained *out there* he was more than happy to keep me afloat.

CASS. I still don't understand.

RONNIE. Because PhD or no PhD, at least I was still in *Israel* – and no matter how hopeless and bloody the country gets, simply being in Israel still counts for something back here among the folks who aren't. In Israel he could still pass me off as a success to friends and family.

CASS. You think that's what it signalled?

* *naches* – joy.

RONNIE. Until that moment I never realised what a godsent opportunity September the 13th 1993 must've seemed to them.

CASS. September 13th – ?

RONNIE. 1993. A few weeks before my thirtieth birthday. I'd been driving a bus for a couple of months, remember?

CASS. I remember how pompous you looked in the *optional* cap you *chose* to wear.

RONNIE. Finsbury Park to Battersea. Battersea to Finsbury Park. Backwards and forwards trying to decide what to do with the rest of my life.

CASS. So?

RONNIE. Mum and dad were aware I was going through some kind of crisis. Though there's no way of knowing for certain that I was invited over *deliberately,* the spread laid on for the occasion should've warned me.

CASS. What occasion?

RONNIE (*impatiently*). September the 13th 1993.

CASS. The more you say it like I'm stupid for not knowing what you're talking about, the more I want to rupture your other kidney.

RONNIE. On September 13th 1993 the Israelis and Palestinians signed the Declaration of Principles on the White House lawn, and the Middle East peace process moved into a new and stupendously optimistic phase.

CASS. Oh. That.

RONNIE. The Oslo Accords – otherwise known as 'oh that'. Mum and dad asked me over to watch the signing ceremony with them. Share a little bit of history. Peace at last. The light unto nations was aglow once more. Or so we were led to believe at the time.

CASS. Was that '93? Thought it was longer for some reason.

RONNIE. Tell it to the Palestinians in the occupied territories . . .

CASS. I would, only I don't go into them quite as often as I'd like. Now if they could set up a Palestinian camp in the car park at Brent Cross, I swear, you'd have to beat me back with tear gas.

RONNIE (*his humour dropping*). Anyone who'd spent even two minutes at an Israeli checkpoint would never make such a crass remark.

CASS. Christ, Ronnie. It was meant to be a joke.

RONNIE. Yeah. Only it's not. Is it?

Pause. RONNIE *takes a hard draw on his cigarette.*

CASS. So why would mum and dad 'deliberately' ask you over that day? What are you getting at?

RONNIE. The suggestion I up sticks and actually go out there to study came the evening of the signing, or shortly after.

CASS. Is that so odd? You were looking for direction. Israel's always been a place for people in search of some kind of permanence. They were crudely matchmaking. They'd never have suggested going during the Intifada because of safety fears. But when Arafat and Rabin shook hands maybe they just thought – in their rather sweet naiveté – that it would also be the fresh start you needed.

RONNIE. Exactly. Studying in Israel. And if the study doesn't work out, there's always Israel itself. Like I said. A godsend.

Beat.

Until, that is, I decide to come home. With nothing. Not even a tan.

CASS (*cautiously*). Mum thinks all it would take for dad to start talking to you is a simple apology.

RONNIE. So that's why you wanted to see me. I was beginning to wonder.

CASS. That's not why I wanted to see you.

RONNIE. Obviously mum couldn't ask me directly. Even though she sleeps the other side of my bedroom wall, far better chance of a result by sending an influential envoy.

ACT ONE 45

CASS. Mum didn't ask me to come up here.

RONNIE. Quite the shuttle diplomat, aren't we?

CASS. I came to ask you about Dan.

RONNIE (*incredulous*). An apology for what? Fuck's sake, Cass – when we were kids how many nights were we put to bed with the story of the Zionist pioneers who turned an empty desert into a garden?

CASS (*trying to keep up*). Sorry – where's this coming from?

RONNIE. Or the Jews' miraculous triumph over the Brits in '47 and the Arabs in '48?

CASS. I don't see what any of this has got to do with what we've just been talking about?

RONNIE (*rolling over her*). Or the prowess of her pilots in '67? The villainy of '72?

CASS. One person firing dates at another person isn't the same as an actual *conversation*, Ronnie. What's your *point*?

RONNIE. Or '73? Or Entebbe? *Apologise*?!

CASS. Are you saying none of that's true?

RONNIE. It's *all* true, but that's not the same as it being the *whole* truth. We were deliberately fed the edited highlights. They sent me out on half the story, and when I discovered the other half for myself, everything fell apart. *Apologise*?

CASS. They had a full-time clothing business to run. Maybe edited highlights were all they had time for. Perhaps they assumed we'd fill in the background for ourselves. We were smart enough, perhaps we should have.

RONNIE. We were children. Jews were the cowboys, Arabs the Indians. That's how basic the level of programming.

CASS. *Programming*? Ronnie, they're not historians. They've never been political. They make cheap, snazzy outfits for large, snazzy women. *Programming*? Give me a fucking break.

RONNIE. They had a duty as parents to make us informed.

CASS. Oh now that's just absurd. Their duty as far as they were concerned was to keep us fed, happy, and in broad agreement with their view of the world as gleaned from the *Daily Express*, the *Mail on Sunday*, and the *Jewish Chronicle*. Anything extra was down to us. They'd lay down their lives for me and you, Ronnie – you know they would.

RONNIE. Don't dive into sentiment to avoid my point!

CASS. I'm not avoiding your point – I just think you're rather shamefully manufacturing a position from which you can accuse mum and dad of deliberately abetting your dissolution. All so you won't have to *abase* yourself with an apology for screwing up an opportunity they underwrote with a *completely* open hand!

RONNIE (*adamant – his bottom line*). I don't believe that. I'm sorry. Not completely open. If they don't like what happened to me over there, so be it. But whether they like it or not they had more than a 'completely open' hand in it. So as far as I'm concerned, I have *nothing* to apologise to them about.

CASS. In their mind it would seem you do, but maybe you're right. Maybe you don't. It doesn't matter.

RONNIE. It matters to me.

CASS. It doesn't matter because the real question is: how much will it actually cost you to do the big thing and just settle this?

RONNIE. It's not about being big, Cass.

CASS. Isn't it?

RONNIE. It's not about *settling* something.

CASS. What is it about?

RONNIE. It's about being *right*.

CASS *cannot move this further. She stands, tired from the fray. Pause.*

CASS (*quieter – a different tack*). You always enjoyed arguing more than I did, and I really didn't ask you up here for an argument.

Beat.

I asked you to meet me to talk about Dan . . .

RONNIE. I don't wanna talk about Dan.

CASS. You and Danny have always talked about each other's girlfriends.

RONNIE. Not for years. I'm tired.

CASS. You've known him longer than anyone. And now I'm the girlfriend.

RONNIE. Tell mum to expect nothing. I'll call you.

RONNIE *starts to walk away.*

CASS (*her anxiety suddenly exploding*). Please, Ronnie! It's a simple question.

RONNIE *stops.*

(*Getting herself under control.*) I just need to know I'm the one.

Beat.

Am I the one, Ronnie? Or am I merely Dan's *next* one?

CASS *looks at* RONNIE*'s back. Pause.* RONNIE *walks off.*

After a few moments, night turns to muted morning sunlight, as DAN *walks onto the scene holding a spindle of twine which disappears into the sky.* DAN *looks up at his kite.* CASS *watches* DAN *for a few moments, then stands and slowly exits.*

DAN. The next one in the range was so big that Cass had visions of Oscar being lifted off the ground.

RONNIE *walks on behind him in shirtsleeves.*

RONNIE. It's certainly more appropriate than the car. But do you know he actually *likes* kites?

DAN. Not sure he's ever seen one. But Cass got the idea from a friend's husband, who's apparently a big enthusiast.

RONNIE. And what do you think about that?

DAN. What do I think about what?

RONNIE. Well . . . that she's getting increasingly involved with Oscar.

DAN. She's given him a kite, Ronnie. Not a scoop of bone marrow.

RONNIE. Even so. I know the extent of her involvement with Oscar is one of Cass's concerns. Perhaps buying the kite is a signal she's coming to terms with the idea.

DAN. I'm taking the fact that she's thinking about him at all as a positive sign.

RONNIE. Sure. Though.

Beat.

No.

DAN. What?

RONNIE. I don't want to be negative. Only, isn't it also possible you're clutching at straws in the absence of anything more concrete?

DAN (*looking up at the sky*). Go on.

RONNIE. Well, she now knows you've been thinking ahead to a time when she might move in with you.

Beat.

And yet she still hasn't expressed the desire to make that a reality from her end.

DAN. I get a sense she's thinking things through.

RONNIE. Well . . . of course, she's had a lot of failed relationships. As you know.

DAN (*looking at the kite*). Uhuh.

RONNIE. So I've started to wonder if my sister's actually cut out for the long haul at all. We used to joke about it, remember?

DAN. When we were kids.

RONNIE. And when we weren't.

DAN (*looking at* RONNIE). What're you getting at?

RONNIE. You know how Cass likes to examine every decision from every angle. In her heart I'm convinced she thinks she's looking for reassurance about a relationship's viability. But in her head I've begun to wonder if she's not actually looking for an escape hatch, should the need arise.

RONNIE *lights up a cigarette and takes a drag.* DAN *looks at* RONNIE. *Beat.*

DAN. Escape?

RONNIE. She told me last week I should move out of my parents.

DAN. She told me too. I agree.

RONNIE. I told her I couldn't until me and the old man had resolved some fundamental differences.

DAN. She's really worried your attempt at resolution could blow up in everyone's face.

RONNIE. Did Cass mention that three days after our conversation up here she left a message for me to call her at work?

DAN (*looking back up at the kite*). She might've.

RONNIE. Seems her boss has been talking on and off for a while about developing some kind of documentary series around episodes of mass hysteria.

DAN. I suppose it's 1999 and all that. Total eclipse of the sun in a couple of months. Millennium and the possible end of the world at the end of the year. Her boss apparently likes things with a topical edge.

RONNIE. They thought they'd probably missed the boat, but then Cass showed this woman –

DAN. Her boss's name is Helen.

RONNIE. Until Cass showed this Helen a tiny section of my unfinished thesis, where I talk a little bit about a phenomenon called the Jerusalem Syndrome.

DAN (*not really paying attention*). Right . . .

RONNIE. When I rang the office, Cass told me she'd persuaded this Helen person that – late in the day as it might be – having me have a crack at a research treatment might be worth a punt.

DAN. Congratulations mate. Great.

RONNIE. Great and more to the point . . . money in my pocket.

DAN. More to the point?

RONNIE. At the moment I have no money, so it's relatively easy to stay at the parents. If this proposal secures me some sort of advance, well. Then I'll have the means to find and fund my own accommodation, and no reason to stay at mum and dad's. I'll have to leave – and sooner rather than later. Bingo.

DAN. Bingo?

RONNIE. Cass's concern about the family imploding is avoided. Which brings us to you.

DAN. Me? How does all that bring us on to me?

RONNIE. We all think Cass is deciding about the future, but perhaps – and this is just a thought – but perhaps she's actually already decided.

DAN. Has she said something?

RONNIE. No, but that doesn't mean anything.

DAN. She would've told me.

RONNIE. How do you tell someone you really care about that perhaps you don't care about them quite as much as you thought?

DAN. But.

RONNIE. Or indeed . . . quite as much as you need if you're to fully commit?

DAN (*beat*). Hang on.

RONNIE. If you're about to ask when is she planning to come clean with you, I can't help you.

DAN. I wasn't.

RONNIE. All I know is a state of protracted hiatus – by definition – can't be dragged out forever. Though it can be spun out until the right time.

DAN. Which would be when exactly?

RONNIE. When the impact of her 'thanks but no thanks' to moving in could be softened by something that would lessen both the blow for you, and the guilt for her.

DAN. You what?

RONNIE. A time when – for example – and this is just theory. This is pure conjecture. But until such time as I might be in a physical and *financial* position to move back into my old room at the flat.

Pause. RONNIE *waits for this to sink in.*

DAN. You're suggesting.

Beat.

You're suggesting.

Pause.

You're suggesting Cass is –

RONNIE. Not 'is', Dan. Not 'is'. 'Might be'. Pure conjecture, remember.

DAN. You're suggesting your sister *might be* holding off telling me we're finished until she's engineered you out of your parents' and back into the flat.

RONNIE. The mind of *Woman*, Daniel. If they could equal our strength and cruelty I firmly believe they would have us in stalls, like pigs, milking our nuts, like cows.

Long pause.

DAN. Hang on.

RONNIE. Think about it. I'm liberated from my parents. She's liberated herself from you. You're liberated from uncertainty. In one light it almost assumes the appearance of a grand humanitarian gesture.

DAN. I said *hang on*.

RONNIE. Perhaps you'd like me to run through the analysis again?

DAN. If Cassie's biding her time to let me down gently, why would she give me this at the weekend?

With his free hand he takes a silver fountain pen from his inside jacket pocket and holds it up.

Beat.

RONNIE. A fountain pen.

DAN. The inscription *on* the pen.

RONNIE. Inscription?

DAN. 'With love always, Cass.'

RONNIE stares at the pen as CASS and HELEN walk to a standstill around the park benches, leaning on them for support. Their faces flushed and sweaty.

RONNIE (*beat*). So the pen would be a sop to buy the time she needs to manoeuvre all the pieces into alignment. *With love always.* What does that actually mean? I'll always love Django Reinhardt, but doesn't mean I'm never going to buy someone else's records. You can love *always* with passion like a lover. Or in fond regret, like an *ex*.

The two women just about regain their breath when LOU limps onto the scene – her jogging bottoms soaking wet, and very muddy.

LOU. Whose idea was it to jump that fucking stream?!

CASS. I chose the route, if that's what you mean.

LOU. There isn't enough terra firma out here you had to seek out vast rivers to leap over?

HELEN. It was hardly a *vast* river. Barely more than a trickle.

LOU. But with embankments of mud in which you could stage *Journey's Fucking End*.

HELEN. Cassie and I jumped it.

ACT ONE   53

LOU (*beat. Pointing at* CASS). Next time *you* run at the rear.

LOU *sits at a bench and takes out a mobile phone.*

CASS. What're you doing?

LOU. What any sane woman would do in this situation – ringing my husband to pick me up.

LOU *stands and crosses upstage to make the call.* DAN *and* RONNIE *regard each other as before.*

DAN (*calm, measured, icily certain*). Listen to me very carefully. You're not getting your old room back. If your sister rules out any possibility of moving in with me . . . you're not getting your old room back. If my teaching contract is torn up tomorrow and I'm suddenly desperate for a tenant . . . you're not getting your old room back. Four years ago you upped and left to be a part of modern history. You did what you felt you had to do. It was bloody difficult for me, but now I'm glad, because it forced me to step out of the glorified playground of our twenties and find a life. I stopped kidding myself I was Fellini, and got a job. I found someone. Married her. Had a kid with her. And even though we eventually broke up, I learned how to maintain relations with her for the sake of my son. In short, your departure was the making of me, and now I have Cass I have no intention of becoming unmade again by you, or anyone else.

HELEN. For what it's worth, Cassie . . . I think your route was fine.

CASS. Thanks.

HELEN. Nicely varied. Plenty of up as well as down. Just the right degree of flat.

DAN. And before I forget. I'm not your fucking sorting office.

DAN *takes out a blue airmail letter and tosses it at* RONNIE'*s feet.*

RONNIE. I gave your address because –

DAN. I know why you gave my address. Your mistake.

LOU *returns to the other two women, putting her mobile away.*

LOU. He's on his way.

CASS *looks out over the view of the city.* HELEN *regards her.*

HELEN (*to* CASS). Is it working?

CASS. Sorry?

HELEN. Jogging. Is it having the desired effect?

CASS. It's too early to say.

LOU. If the desired effect is to convince me to exercise in a luxury gym before a large, noisy telly, then categorically, *yes*.

HELEN. I suggested jogging would help clear her mind.

LOU. Of what?

CASS. Helen thought it might help clarify my thoughts about Danny and Ronnie. The open parkland. Fresh air.

DAN. Why did you come back, Ron?

HELEN. Cassie told me what's been going on between her, Dan, and brother Ronnie. And that she didn't know what to make of it all. So I said 'jog'.

CASS. Helen believes my various anxieties are different expressions of the same thing.

HELEN. An elemental crisis.

DAN. Why didn't you just stay out there?

LOU. An elemental crisis?

HELEN. Of trust, which jogging could help bring into focus.

LOU. An elemental crisis of trust solved by *jogging*?

HELEN. Unlike room-based exercise, jogging forces us to become creatures of environment once more. Out in the open the self-serving rationalizations of the cosmopolitan metropolitan give way to more primary desires and anxieties.

LOU. And Cass is a cosmopolitan metropolitan, is she?

HELEN. What do I *want*? What do I *need*? That sort of thing.

LOU (*sarcastically*). Cool.

CASS. Helen produced an extremely well-received series scrutinizing contemporary relationships.

LOU. Is that right?

CASS. Award-winning.

LOU. Congratulations.

HELEN. Thank you.

RONNIE. Dan, let me just say one thing –

DAN (*cutting him off, quiet, resolved*). I don't think so. My days of listening to you are over. I'm going to take what's written on Cass's pen at face value, and then I'm going to carry on and hope for the best.

RONNIE. Hope for the best?

DAN. Who was it who said when you lose hope you die.

RONNIE. That would be Martin Luther King.

DAN. Well then.

RONNIE. He also said freedom is never voluntarily given by the oppressor, it must be demanded by the oppressed. For which he – like several other men of peace – was rewarded with a Nobel Prize and a bullet in the chest.

DAN. I'll take my chances.

CASS. All I want to know is, am I the one?

RONNIE. You're living in a dream, Daniel.

CASS. Am I the one? Or am I merely his next one?

DAN. If anyone's living in a dream, it's you.

The kite now packed away, DAN *pockets* CASS*'s pen, and walks offstage.*

RONNIE *hesitates for a moment, then picks up the airmail letter. He slips the letter into a pocket, and walks away down the hill in the opposite direction.*

LOU *waves at* DOUGLAS *offstage and exits in his general direction, while* CASS *remains on a bench as* HELEN *stretches, limbering up.*

The sound of London rises – the background growl of traffic; aeroplanes overhead; trains rolling past; birds; mopeds; children. Comforting everyday noise of contemporary London.

Slow fade to black.

ACT TWO

A roof garden in inner-city London, overlooking tightly-packed housing of the area.

The morning of August 11th, 1999. A sturdy tripod stands in the centre of the roof. At its base lies a relatively small cardboard box. Around the perimeter of the area lies the remote-controlled car on its side, the kite, with its twine unravelled and dumped in a heap on top, and a deflated leather Arsenal football – in addition to a host of forgotten and broken toys discarded by OSCAR.

After a few moments, DAN *carefully reverses onto the roof with* DOUGLAS, *each holding an end of the tubular body of an astronomical telescope, which they carry carefully over to the tripod – and then just as carefully lower it to the floor beside it.*

DOUGLAS. The beauty of a kite, of course, is its portability.

DAN. Portability wasn't his mother's issue. His mother's issue was a three-year-old standing around in a cold wind holding a piece of string.

DOUGLAS. Goes with the territory, I'm afraid.

DAN. I was up for it. And I think Oscar was, in the way they'll go along with anything at that age.

DOUGLAS. Mother's prerogative to worry about her child, Dan.

DAN. Within reason worry is more than reasonable.

DOUGLAS. Within reason?

DAN. First it was the cold, then the wind chill factor, then exposure to rain, and then sun. *Then* the possibility of permanent damage to his neck from looking up too much. And finally, an all-consuming anxiety that the thing could plummet from a hundred feet, point down, directly onto his still-hardening skull.

DOUGLAS. I've only seen that happen once in twenty years of kite-flying.

DAN. I told her if it happened every day they'd ban it.

DOUGLAS. The girl was back on her feet within . . . I'm not exactly sure . . . a week, two tops. Minimal indentation. Slight permanent hair loss along the line of impact. But nothing that wouldn't become the basis for an amusing party anecdote later in life.

DAN. I told her the chance of Oscar being impaled on his own kite was like, very, very small to minute. But when she delivered the ultimatum that he either goes to the park in a crash helmet or not at all I thought, you know . . . fuckit. Life is for living, even at three-and-a-half.

DOUGLAS. Especially at three-and-a-half.

DAN. If it was up to her she'd swathe him in bubble wrap and embed him in concrete for ten years.

DOUGLAS (*beat*). Astronomy's an interesting compromise.

DAN. Too many people on the planet with an outlook no further than the nearest switch. I want to ensure my boy grows up at least aware of 'outside'.

DOUGLAS (*apropos the telescope*). A lot of outside to be aware of with this.

DAN. That's the beauty. An interest for life.

DOUGLAS. For sure.

DAN. Had the idea when I took him to the Planetarium over Easter. Didn't really have a clue what was going on, of course, except he twigged it went on outside. So I start him off with something big and obvious like the Moon, and gradually expand his horizon as he gets older.

DOUGLAS. Oscar's a lucky boy.

DAN. Don't know about that.

DOUGLAS. Shame he couldn't be here for the eclipse.

DAN. His mother suddenly produced pre-booked tickets for some cartoon shite at the pictures. Deliberate. Terrified he'll blind himself by accident, so she makes sure he can't by hiding him in a windowless black box when it all goes down. Or up.

DOUGLAS. Or across.

DAN. Exactly.

DOUGLAS. Perhaps he'll catch the next one.

DAN. If he still has his sight when he's ninety-five.

DAN crouches and opens the cardboard box and unpacks a small array of smaller boxes. DOUGLAS watches.

So where is little chummy? Cass was rather hoping you'd bring her over.

DOUGLAS. We left her at home with a box of matches and a large bottle of lighter fluid.

DAN (*not paying attention*). Right . . .

He stops unpacking the small boxes, and freezes for a moment.

DOUGLAS (*beat*). When she keeps me up for more than three nights my paternal instinct turns murderous. No – chummy's with my mother. Hands like oven mitts, eyes like an endoscope, mind like a health and safety manual.

DAN rolls the body of the telescope over, and pulls the tripod down to attach it.

DAN. Could you . . . ? ((*Indicating* DOUGLAS *should hold the tripod steady upside down – which he does.*) Between you and me I think Cass was hoping a baby's presence would take her mind off it.

DOUGLAS (*helping* DAN *attach the telescope to the tripod*). Off what?

DAN. This little gathering.

DOUGLAS. But it's just friends on the roof going 'ooh' in awe.

DAN. Didn't Louise tell you?

DOUGLAS. That depends. Lou keeps me informed about things on a don't need to know basis.

The telescope is now screwed onto the tripod. DAN *stands and bends to pick it up.*

DAN. So you don't know.

DOUGLAS *helps set the tripod and telescope on its legs.*

DOUGLAS. I work for the Inland Revenue, Dan. I'm really not very good at elliptical.

DAN. About me finally asking Cass to move in.

DOUGLAS. Oh that.

DAN. So you *do* know?

DOUGLAS. Lou must have let something slip in her sleep.

DAN *unpacks a couple of viewfinders (coarse and crosshair) from the smaller of the boxes and carefully fits them to the telescope.*

I'm still in the dark why Cass would be nervous about having a few people over?

DAN (*looking into the eyepiece and making an adjustment*). We've never entertained here as a couple before.

DOUGLAS. Hardly entertaining. No offence, but these are clothes I wear for gardening.

DAN. The point is – it's like Cass and I on show in the flat for the first time. At least I'm guessing that's it. She won't talk about it, but she's been jittery all morning. Hardly slept. I didn't want to push it, because pushing edgy women usually makes things worse.

DOUGLAS (*from experience*). Oh yes.

DAN. But I think it's like, this is it. Grown up time. People coming over. Can we manage? Are we the real McCoy as a couple?

DOUGLAS. But I'm assuming it's all people she knows.

DAN. You and Lou. Ronnie and Helen.

DOUGLAS. Helen?

DAN. Cass's boss.

DOUGLAS. I met her when she was jogging with Lou and Cass on the heath. Lou had spectacularly failed to hurdle a small puddle and I was summoned to salvage the wreckage. You've met her?

DAN. Spoken to on the 'phone once or twice but not met. Very smart producer according to Cass. Very sharp.

DOUGLAS. I couldn't say. I only saw her in skin-tight leggings and a figure-hugging crop top.

DAN. And?

DOUGLAS *smiles*.

I hear you.

DOUGLAS. I'm a married man with a young child, Dan. You hear *nothing*.

LOU *comes onto the roof, followed by* CASS, *holding two glasses of white wine – which she hands to* DOUGLAS *and* DAN.

LOU. Is that a telescope on your roof, or are you just pleased to see me?

DOUGLAS. It's a telescope on the roof.

CASS. Dan. Helen's here.

LOU (*in* DOUGLAS's *ear*). A tad over-dressed for a solar eclipse in my opinion. But then I don't work in television – where every gathering of two or more people is a potential career move.

HELEN *comes onto the roof, watched by the others. She is very smartly dressed – powerful but chic. She crosses directly to* DAN, *extending her hand*.

CASS. Dan this is Helen. Helen this is Dan.

HELEN. Hello, Danny.

DAN (*shaking her hand*). Nice to finally put a face to the name.

HELEN (*shaking it back*). You too.

LOU (*to* HELEN). My husband –

DOUGLAS. Douglas.

LOU (*to* HELEN). – you've met.

> HELEN *regards* DOUGLAS *for a moment, unsure when and where.*

HELEN. Um . . . ?

DOUGLAS (*extending his hand*). On the heath. My wife tripped over a leaf, and I airlifted her to a large bar of chocolate.

LOU. Douglas is the Inland Revenue's leading stand-up comedian. His wit has a small but loyal following within tax officialdom, but we're not sure how it translates beyond the world of the un-dead.

HELEN (*shaking his hand*). Good to see you again, Douglas.

DOUGLAS. Call me Doug.

LOU. He thinks it makes him sound vaguely antipodean.

DOUGLAS *(to* HELEN). It's simply less of a mouthful.

LOU. Helen's mouth looks suitably wide, Douglas. I'm sure she can manage.

DAN (*to* CASS). No sign of Ronnie?

CASS. My brother knows what time the eclipse starts, like everyone else in the hemisphere.

DAN. I don't know why you asked him.

CASS. I asked him because I want to speak to him.

LOU. How is Ronnie? The last you told me he'd been commissioned to put together some kind of document based on his travels.

HELEN. Just a small paper about the Jerusalem Syndrome.

DOUGLAS (*his ears pricking up*). The Jerusalem Syndrome?

HELEN. You did tell him a page and a half would be enough to begin with didn't you, Cassie?

CASS. Of course.

LOU. What's the Jerusalem Syndrome when it's at home? Though I'm guessing its home is Jerusalem.

HELEN. I'll be in a better position to inform you once I've read Ronnie's paper.

DOUGLAS. The Jerusalem Syndrome is a phenomenon often – though not exclusively – associated with the end of millennia.

LOU. Yes, thank you, Douglas, but I was asking Helen.

DOUGLAS. Devout Christians in Jerusalem occasionally experience a disparity between their mental image of the ancient city, and the realities of a modern metropolis.

LOU. I said I was asking Helen.

DOUGLAS. I know what you said. In addition, particularly religious Jews with the syndrome may believe that the building of the third temple is imminent, that the ancient animal sacrifices will be restored, and that their own Messiah will arrive shortly. It's a delusive condition whose origins date back as far as 1033.

Beat.

I heard a feature on Radio Four.

DOUGLAS *smiles at* LOU *and takes a sip of wine.* LOU *fumes. Pause.*

HELEN. If we can submit a proposal before the next commissioning round, we could be greenlit by Christmas.

LOU. That sounds painful.

DAN. I'm going downstairs for a refill, before the light fades and the birds go berserk.

LOU. I'm sure we'll stay perfectly calm.

DOUGLAS (*indicating the sky*). I think Dan is referring to the period when the moon passes in front of the sun, and the birds will –

LOU. – think it's dusk and bed down for the night. Yes, Douglas. I *know*.

DOUGLAS. Good for you.

DAN. Anyone's glass need refreshing?

DOUGLAS. I wouldn't mind.

DAN. Follow me.

DAN and DOUGLAS go inside. Beat.

CASS (*to* LOU). You two are on form.

LOU (*to* HELEN). Some marriages are built on romantic slush – we've chosen mouth-to-mouth combat as our stimulant of choice.

HELEN. Right. Cassie, could I have a word. (*To* LOU.) Excuse us.

LOU. She didn't say 'yes'.

HELEN. I'm her boss – the question was rhetorical.

HELEN leads CASS a little away from LOU.

He will deliver, won't he? It's been four weeks. I'm not exactly asking for *The Ascent of Man*.

CASS. He gave his word.

HELEN. It would be a shame if he took the money and ran, because I really think that we could be in with a shot with it.

CASS. I've explained to him what a terrific opportunity it would be to get things back on track.

HELEN. Things?

CASS. His life.

HELEN. We're a television production company, Cassie, not Battersea dog's home.

CASS. I know.

HELEN. I hate to see ideas of real potential taken away from the people who bring them in. But you know I will if I have to.

CASS. What do you think of Dan?

HELEN. Nicer than you described.

CASS. I didn't want to overdo the lavish description in case it unduly affected your line of approach. What's your first impression?

HELEN. I would. Definitely. If I did men anymore. Which I don't.

CASS. I meant of his, of you.

HELEN. It's difficult to be precise about these things. But dilated pupils, moist, parted lips, strong handshake, subliminal self-grooming during open conversation – I'd say it was a solid start.

CASS. I don't know. I'm not sure this is such a good idea.

HELEN. Relax, Cassie. All things come to those who –

LOU (*her eye at the telescope*). Oh my word . . . !

CASS and HELEN turn to LOU, who is looking through the telescope, now pointed out front.

CASS (*looking into the sky, shielding her eyes*). Has it started?

LOU. Flats over there. About ten floors up. Old geezer on balcony. *Completely starkers!*

CASS (*peering into the middle distance*). Where?

HELEN (*also peering, entirely matter of fact*). Oh yes.

LOU. You can't possibly see unaided.

HELEN (*peering*). Uncircumcised.

LOU looks into the eyepiece. Beat.

LOU. That's *incredible*. Was your mother by any chance fertilised by a hawk?

HELEN. I've always been long-sighted. Show me a ten inch penis three feet away and all I'll register is an unfeasibly long blur. But at distance, everything comes out clear as crystal.

CASS. I can barely see the block of flats let alone his block and tackle.

HELEN *moves behind* CASS, *and takes her head in both hands and re-directs her line of sight.*

HELEN. There.

CASS. Without my glasses everything beyond the edge of this roof is basically a blur.

HELEN (*still holding* CASS*'s head in her hands*). I didn't know that.

CASS. Ronnie's the same.

LOU. If he doesn't turn up soon he'll miss it. From here, at least.

CASS. He's probably tied up at mum and dad's.

LOU. What's the situation there at the moment?

CASS. Not good.

LOU. No?

CASS. After the big freeze came the little thaw, followed shortly after by the enormous heated argument.

LOU. Doesn't sound very promising.

CASS. What began as an encouragingly well-behaved opening dialogue about Ronnie's conduct in Israel, rapidly degenerated into a slanging match about Israel itself – with dad insisting on its right to do whatever it needs, to protect itself, and Ronnie insisting that the only real threat comes from Israel's treatment of the Palestinians, and increasing numbers of settlements in the occupied territories.

HELEN. Whenever that issue comes up on the news I tend to switch over. I just find it too . . .

Long pause, while CASS *and* LOU *wait for* HELEN *to find the appropriate word. They wait for what seems like an age.*

. . . boring, I suppose.

CASS (*beat*). They've been going at it hammer and tongs, according to mum.

HELEN. Not to mention depressing.

ACT TWO   67

LOU (*trying to ignore* HELEN). Josie's caught in the middle?

CASS. She generally follows dad's line, but I think she just wants them to stop fighting.

LOU. Of course.

CASS. It seems Ronnie dropped out of his PhD after falling in with some young radicals, apparently only too pleased to befriend an impressionable young Jew from the West. Claiming to be disaffected with the leadership of both sides –

LOU. *Claiming* to be?

CASS. I'm giving you my parents' take on what happened.

LOU. Right. Sorry. Go on.

CASS. So claiming to be disaffected with both Israeli and Palestinian leaders, they seemed to have convinced my brother that winning over foreign opinion was central to their objective of highlighting human rights abuses. Dad's guessing they took Ronnie under their wing, showed him lots of emotive photographs of shot children, pumped him full of propaganda, and sent him home to spread the word.

LOU. Going by what I've read in the papers their word is pretty compelling.

CASS. That rather depends on *which* journalists in *which* papers.

LOU. I suppose.

CASS. Anyway, they came across a letter sent to Ronnie by the brother of some young Palestinian woman from the West Bank – who dad's rather feverishly decided was used as some kind of sexual lure.

HELEN. How exciting!

CASS. It's all become horribly messy. With Ronnie regurgitating all manner of horror stories about the territories, and Dad trying to shout him down.

LOU. What I know of your father, I'm assuming his views on that area are pretty solid.

CASS. He's supported Israel from before the beginning.

LOU. Sure.

CASS. Why should he take lectures from Ronnie?

LOU. No, of course. But having a view on the occupied territories is hardly the same as attacking the foundations of Zionism, Cass. I mean, I know I'm not Jewish, but –

CASS. Not *occupied* territories.

LOU. Sorry?

CASS. *Disputed.* A change in status effectively conceded by Yasser Arafat at Oslo, as part of a deal accepting *partial* as opposed to *complete* withdrawal of Israel from the West Bank and Gaza, as specified by United Nations resolution 242 of November 22nd, 1967.

LOU. Right.

CASS. I've been boning up.

LOU (*beat*). I know I know virtually nothing. But all I meant before in regard to the occupied – sorry, *disputed* territories –

HELEN. I'd drop it if I were you.

LOU. Sorry?

HELEN. Fucking minefield.

LOU. But I'm allowed to have an opinion.

HELEN. Are you Jewish?

LOU. I think I already said I wasn't.

HELEN. Are you Palestinian?

LOU. Patently not.

HELEN. Then what would your opinion actually be *worth*?

LOU (*bridling*). I beg your pardon?

CASS. Helen's right, Lou. It is a fucking minefield. Now's probably not the time.

LOU *looks at* CASS, *who smiles. Pause.*

LOU. I think I'll go and let Doug's mother know we arrived safely.

CASS. The 'phone's on the wall in the front room.

LOU. It's okay. Doug's got his mobile.

CASS (*looking at her watch, calling after her*). Tell them it's not long to go. *Minutes*, Lou!

LOU goes inside. Pause. HELEN *crosses to the telescope and looks through the eyepiece.* CASS *seems edgier than before.*

I'm having massive second thoughts.

HELEN. Don't. Every woman featured in the series had exactly the same anxiety as you're now experiencing. But when they received the result. For those whose fears *were* founded and those whose fears *weren't* . . . the relief of *knowing* was overwhelming.

CASS. But they had more reason to doubt than I have. You just said yourself how very nice Dan seems.

HELEN. The days of skipping hand in hand to the promised land with a partner for life are over, Cassie. We no longer have to subject ourselves to leaps of faith about the people we spend our lives with. Some see this as a problem. Not me. I say let's be modern and judge the world by what we see – not by what we might wish to see. It's been a long road, but if women are finally learning better than to take men on trust, so be it. Isn't that why those poor cows on the documentary put themselves through the ordeal?

CASS. Yes, but –

HELEN. Isn't this why your eyes widened like saucers when I gave you the tape to watch? It's not how nice they *seem*. It's how trustworthy they *are*.

CASS. It feels like entrapment.

HELEN. Who was it who said he has the profile of a serial monogamist? Not me.

CASS. I just need to know I'm –

HELEN. – the one, and not just the next one. And why not? And this is how. It's not exact, but it will give you a robust pointer to help you make up your mind about Dan once and for all.

HELEN crosses to CASS and stands a couple of feet from her. She puts a hand reassuringly on her arm.

I like you, Cassie. You should be happy. I can see in your eyes that you're worried about the duplicity. Don't be. It's in Danny's interest as well as yours. It protects all parties.

CASS. Except you.

HELEN. Some women do this for a living. The peace of mind of a good friend is the only reward I seek.

CASS. But are you *sure* you can do this?

HELEN (*smiling*). You think I've never done this before?

Long pause. HELEN holds out her empty glass.

Send Danny up with a pair of safety specs. Tell him in my excitement I'm threatening to stare at the sun unprotected.

Pause. CASS regards HELEN, who regards her back

(*Gently.*) It isn't about the man you know, Cass. It's about the man you don't.

Beat. CASS regards HELEN for a moment longer and then takes her glass. She then returns inside. HELEN watches her, and then takes a compact from her jacket and refreshes her lipstick and make-up. HELEN puts her compact away and shades her eyes with her hand and looks up at the sky.

The sky almost imperceptibly starts to darken. A few city lights far and near automatically flicker on, as DAN appears on the roof holding a pair of black safety specs used for looking at the eclipse.

Pause.

DAN. Cass said you wanted to get a head start on the rest of us.

HELEN doesn't turn, but stands with her back to DAN, shading her eyes.

HELEN (*pointing*). Were you aware that you are overlooked by an old-age exhibitionist. 1, 2, 3, 4, 5, 6 . . . 12 floors up over there.

DAN (*looking*). Mm. It's Raoul. (*Waving.*) Raoul! See – he's waving back.

HELEN. Raoul?

DAN. When he used to live here, Cass's brother decided after a bit of a session that the old flasher was Raoul Wallenberg. And don't think the nudity's a summer thing. That's what Raoul wants you to think, so you'll find him endearing and look longer. Summer, autumn, winter, spring. It's all out, all the time.

HELEN *regards* DAN *with mild mystification.*

As Secretary to the Swedish Legation in Budapest, Wallenberg saved a ton of Jews from the Nazis. Non-Jews who helped Jews used to rank among Ronnie's favourite people.

HELEN. And Ronnie thinks that's him?

DAN. No more than I think it's Glen Miller. Raoul was arrested by the Soviets after the war and disappeared. With enough lager down your throat the old perv could also pass for Lord Lucan, Captain Oates, Elvis, and God. In fact . . . just about anyone who vanished without trace a long time ago.

Beat.

Your specs.

HELEN *takes the glasses. Beat.*

HELEN. I like your telescope.

DAN. Thank you. Strictly speaking I bought it for my son as a crude way of spending lots of time together. I was planning to surprise him with it when he comes over tomorrow. But since it was here it I thought we may as well make use of it this once-in-a-lifetime time.

HELEN. Won't it be dangerous?.

DAN. Special filters – super-dark.

HELEN (*beat*). Cassie tells me you're a film-maker, Danny.

DAN. She didn't.

HELEN. Um. Yes. She did.

DAN. I gave up telling people that years ago. I teach media studies. I teach film. I don't make it.

HELEN. But you have done.

DAN. I indulged a fantasy of myself that reality significantly failed to live up to. Cass shouldn't have told you that. Really. Because it's not true.

HELEN (*beat*). I liked *Doors Without Keys* very much.

Pause.

DAN. I'm sorry?

HELEN. I thought you packed into quarter of an hour what many celebrated film-makers scarcely manage in their entire careers.

DAN. I'm sorry, but how –

Pause. HELEN *smiles at* DAN.

HELEN. Don't be angry at her, Danny. She only had your interest at heart.

DAN. That chapter of my life is officially closed. It's more than officially closed. It's dead.

HELEN. Perhaps Cassie doesn't think it should be.

DAN. She knows I'm perfectly content with the way my life has panned out.

HELEN. Content? Content is the coward's word for 'resigned'.

DAN. Okay. Listen. I have no ambitions. No illusions. I don't feel the need to compete with anyone. I'm just me. Slightly less stupid than the stupid people I teach. Happy telling them where to look up what I don't know. I have a nice little flat. A reliable little car. An adorable little boy, and I pay all my *little* bills on time.

HELEN. And?

DAN. There is no and. That's it. Why does there always have to be an and?

HELEN. With people of real talent there's always an *and*, Danny. I know how hard it is to find people who'll back an idea. I know how soul-destroying it is to go cap in hand to Philistine Row for what to them is meter-money. The best ones, the real artists, they walk away. While people like me – the blockheads who don't know any better – just keep banging away until the walls of resistance finally crack.

DAN. Cass had no right to give you my tape.

HELEN. She's proud of your work. She had *every* right.

DAN (*floundering a little*). I feel like I'm being disinterred here . . .

HELEN. She knows I can help you.

Pause.

DAN. You can help me – what? Reintroduce failure as the major theme of my life? No offence but no thanks.

HELEN. Whatever you earn as a teacher I could quadruple overnight. After two years double that. Within four you could buy out the other residents of this building, and knock it into your own. How's that for lemons?

DAN. Look. I already told you –

HELEN (*affecting losing patience*). I know what you already told me, Danny. And I'm telling you I think you've embalmed yourself in mediocrity by way of consolation that things didn't take off as soon as you expected. I'm also telling you I can make what I just said – all I just said and more – happen for you. Not as some favour to Cassie. Not out of the goodness of my heart. Because you've *got* something, and so few people have.

Pause. They regard one another. HELEN *puts on her dark safety specs.*

DAN (*quiet, nervous now*). What are you doing?

HELEN. I'm protecting my eyes from your dazzle.

Pause.

DAN. You've seen one film. A single, fifteen-minute film. That's all.

HELEN. There are two more. I know. Cass wanted to bring them to me, but I said uh-uh. I said, Danny has to bring them to me or there's really no point.

HELEN *slowly crosses to* DAN. *She stands in front of him.*

Will you bring them to me, Danny?

Beat.

Shall we meet one evening, and you can introduce them to me before we watch? You could come to the office.

DAN. I don't think –

HELEN. Everyone leaves by seven. I know how self-conscious you'll be. I know how to handle talent, Danny. Believe me. I can be very supportive.

DAN (*beat*). So. Um. Let Cass know when you're free and –

HELEN. You tell me. You. Not little Cassie.

DAN. Not little Cassie?

HELEN. Let's give the researcher the night off.

Pause. DAN *regards* HELEN. *After a few moments* CASS *appears on the roof, and regards* HELEN *and* DAN *– unseen by both.* CASS *comes slowly onto the roof proper.*

CASS. Everyone's coming up for totality.

LOU *and* DOUGLAS *come onto the roof.*

DOUGLAS. You are aware it's not complete totality in London, just –

LOU. – ninety-five per cent. Yes, Doug. We are.

DOUGLAS. I just wouldn't want you to be disappointed.

DAN *and* HELEN *separate and take up places downstage at the opposite ends of the roof.*

DAN. No sign of Ronnie?

LOU. Actually he just buzzed up.

DAN (*close to* CASS). I really don't know why you invited him.

CASS (*close to* DAN). I told you why I invited him. I invited him because I need to speak to him.

DAN (*pulling* CASS *to one side*). Don't you think you've done enough *speaking* to people?

CASS. What's that supposed to mean?

DAN. Your boss has just been telling me about your conversation concerning my history as a maker of films nobody wanted to see.

CASS. Not now, Dan.

DAN. Not now?

HELEN. Look! It's starting!

Everyone turns to the front and looks up.

Almost as one they put on their black safety specs and look up at the sun, as the light gradually dims from crepuscular to almost black, to complete darkness. The twittering birds slowly fall silent.

Pause.

DOUGLAS. There it is . . . the first diamond ring . . .

CASS. It's . . .

DAN (*beat*). Isn't it just.

Pause. In the darkness RONNIE *comes onto the roof.*

RONNIE. Sorry I'm late. Something –

DAN. Sssh.

LOU. I still don't understand how it fits over the sun so completely.

DOUGLAS. Most of the time it doesn't. That's why most of the time we don't get totality. Two minutes of relatively complete occlusion every seventy or so years. Not much when you think of it in those terms.

LOU. Saying I don't understand how it fits completely over the sun is not the same as inviting you to explain how it does.

DOUGLAS. I was attempting to illuminate your darkness.

LOU. When I need my darkness illuminating, I'll buy a torch.

DOUGLAS. I'll come with you. We can pick one out together.

DAN. Sssh!

They all continue to look up at the eclipse. RONNIE *joins them, already wearing his black safety specs. He also looks up.*

Pause.

HELEN. It's quite extraordinary.

DAN. Right now, I feel about yea small.

CASS. Just think, all over the world, right now, whatever people were doing two minutes ago, they've stopped.

Beat.

Working. Eating. Driving.

HELEN. Shagging. Dancing. Singing. Swimming.

DAN. Punching. Shooting. Stabbing. Killing.

LOU. If we agree it's basically all the verbs, can we say that we don't *actually* need to list each and every one?

HELEN. Just imagine, at this very moment, because torturers and murderers are also watching this – fewer people are being tortured or murdered during these two minutes than possibly during any two minutes for seventy-two years.

DOUGLAS. Your assertion needs a little modification, Helen.

HELEN. Does it?

DOUGLAS. Only along the lines of limiting what you've just described to the actual path of the eclipse across northern Europe, the Balkans, etcetera. But in principle, it's a nice thought.

LOU. It was until you modified it to its knees. Occasionally. Just occasionally, Douglas, it would be nice to live in an unqualified moment.

DAN. Look! The corona!

CASS. Oh my word . . . !

They all look in wonder at the corona.

HELEN. That is just gorgeous!

CASS. Gorgeous doesn't even come close.

Pause. They look.

RONNIE (*beat*). Last night I found myself in an internet cafe. As you do.

DAN. Yeah – only we're all looking at this now.

RONNIE. So I log on. As you do.

DAN. Ronnie . . .

RONNIE. And I came across this website which had a poem about the eclipse by a ten-year-old girl. As they do.

DOUGLAS. Quite wonderful.

RONNIE. The girl lives in Ramallah. As she does.

CASS (*suddenly turning*). Ramallah?

RONNIE. And her poem compares what we're watching right now to the light of her people being slowly extinguished –

CASS. Ronnie, shut up!

RONNIE. – by the relentless construction of settlements across –

CASS (*urgent*). *Ronnie!*

RONNIE. – Palestinian territory. Of course, like anything on the net it could've been penned by a trucker from Wigan. But then again. Perhaps not.

Long pause.

DAN (*pissed off*). Thanks, Ronnie . . .

DAN *takes off his safety specs and breaks away from the line, crossing upstage.* CASS *stares at* RONNIE, *still wearing her glasses.*

CASS (*looking directly at* RONNIE). You selfish shit.

DOUGLAS (*still looking up*). Baily's beads!

The light starts to rise, quicker than it dimmed, but not immediately to full daylight. DAN *stands upstage looking at* RONNIE *from behind.*

CASS (*looking directly at* RONNIE). I don't believe you. Not only do you turn up late. But when you do eventually grace us with your presence, you simply can't resist ruining what for most of us would probably have been one of the most memorable moments of our lives.

DAN. It's not worth it.

CASS (*deeply angry*). No, Dan, it fucking is! You don't know what's going on so don't tell me it's not worth it.

RONNIE. I'm so sorry a little bit of unpalatable despair tainted your magic moment everyone. But there really is a limit to the amount of infantile horseshit those of us on *planet Earth* can bear!

CASS. Planet Earth? You?

DAN. What – do you mean I don't know what's going on?

CASS. Please, take our guests downstairs.

DOUGLAS (*the only one still looking and pointing up*). The second diamond ring!

LOU. Doug, it's *over*.

RONNIE. 'Oh look, the sun's gone out – the world's a better place for thirty seconds. Doesn't it just make you *wonder*?' Couldn't possibly occur to you that your torturers and your murderers would actually take the opportunity to stick the boot in all the harder for being *unseen*? That they operate at their peak efficiency with the blinds drawn and the lights off!

CASS. Dan!

DAN. Now?

CASS. It can't wait.

HELEN *crosses to* DAN.

HELEN (*gently*). Why don't we watch the coverage downstairs?

DAN. What's going on, Cass?

HELEN. I hear people are chasing the eclipse in Concorde. Why don't we go and see how the other half blows its cash?

HELEN *gently starts to lead a reluctant* DAN *towards the entrance.*

DAN (*to* RONNIE). I told her you'd spoil it. I told her not to ask you. You've become a spoiler, Ronnie.

RONNIE. Whatever I've become, I'd rather be anything than you!

DAN (*beat*). You see enjoyment. You take out your dick. And you piss all over it.

HELEN. Come on . . .

HELEN *leads* DAN *down.*

LOU (*standing where she was, but talking low*). Douglas?

DOUGLAS (*low*). But we came to watch the eclipse.

LOU (*low but firm*). And now the eclipse is over –

DOUGLAS (*low*). No – *totality's* over. The end of the eclipse *proper* still has a way to go.

CASS. Please, Doug.

DOUGLAS *regards* CASS. *Beat.*

DOUGLAS. When I reached a certain age, and it was time to choose the way I would pass what little time I got to myself, it never entered my head that looking up at sky could get so fucking complicated.

LOU *and* DOUGLAS *also cross to the entrance. With a glance behind them at* CASS *and* RONNIE, LOU *and* DOUGLAS *go downstairs.*

CASS (*to* RONNIE). Have you gone completely insane?

RONNIE. In twenty-four hours you're the second person to ask me that.

CASS. Who was the first?

RONNIE. Dad. Immediately after giving me this.

RONNIE takes off his specs, and reveals a dark new bruise over his left eye.

I know he goes to the gym twice a week, but I assumed it was purely aesthetic. You have to hand it to the *alte kacker*.* Full fist to the socket. No messing. Boom.

CASS. What did you say to him?

RONNIE. What did I say?

CASS. God knows he's no angel, but he would sooner cut off his hands than lay a finger on either of us. You said something to provoke him.

RONNIE. I see. So as long the wrong thing is *said* extreme violence is justified, is it?

Pause.

CASS. Israel.

RONNIE. Extreme violence followed by expulsion.

CASS. Wasn't it?

RONNIE. Mum bawling in the background. I tell him it's five and twenty past midnight. I've nowhere to go. Apparently, that's no longer his concern.

CASS. Where did you sleep?

RONNIE. On the heath – why, is there a room here I could have had?

Beat.

Think I'll join the party downstairs. I need a drink.

RONNIE starts to cross to the entrance.

---

* *alte kacker* – old shitter.

CASS (*a controlled shout*). I didn't ask you here to party! I asked you here to tell you I *know* what you're doing, and it's going to stop!

RONNIE *stops and turns.*

RONNIE (*beat*). 'It'?

CASS. First you sow a seed of doubt in my mind about Dan. Then you sow a seed of doubt in Dan's mind about me. And when that failed to break us up and see you back in your room, you turn plain nasty and start goading mum and dad.

RONNIE. Goading?

CASS. About Israel. Not resolving your issues. The exact opposite.

RONNIE. Not goading. Opening the mind of.

CASS. Dad's mind has been blissfully ajar for most of our lives. Prising it any more open against his will could only succeed in scaring him shitless. He's a simple, essentially decent man looking for a quiet life. But attack him where it matters and he'll dig a trench and take up the position. As well you knew.

RONNIE. As well I knew?

CASS. When you set out to destroy my relationship with your best friend.

RONNIE. *Now* who's insane?

CASS. You couldn't manage it directly, so you set about trying to dismantle the context in which we exist as a couple. Where better to start than the home of my parents?

RONNIE. What?!

CASS. Don't play the dumb innocent with me!

RONNIE. Let's get the others up here. I think they'd love to hear paranoia this riotous . . .

CASS. Israel is central to the parents' sense of themselves. They lived the death of European Jewry and the birth of Israel *first hand*. It was real life to them, not an hour on the

History Channel. A real sanctuary. A real haven. A real miracle built on – and by – blood and guts.

RONNIE. Necessary myth-making aside. Have I *ever* said I didn't respect the moral imperative behind the establishment of the State?

CASS. I don't know what you think any more. You seem to have come back more messed up than you went – which is something of an achievement in itself.

RONNIE. Every realistic Palestinian I spoke to has moved on from that. Nobody likes to be on the losing side of history. What they don't understand is why they have to lose quite this badly for quite this long.

CASS. All I know is by haranguing mum and dad you make them feel threatened at their core. Which gets manifested as a heightened sensitivity towards phenomena they were already struggling to get to grips with.

RONNIE. *Phenomena?*

CASS. Such as seeing their daughter in a serious mixed relationship.

RONNIE. Let me get this straight –

CASS. You know the effect it has. You must! What other reason would you have for creating it?

DAN *appears at the entrance.*

DAN. I heard shouting.

CASS. Go downstairs, Dan.

DAN. Please don't tell me where to go in my own flat.

CASS (*looking at* RONNIE). This is what you want, isn't it? Divide and conquer.

RONNIE. I don't know what you're talking about.

CASS. Up until four days ago mum had always been nothing but affable towards Dan.

DAN. What happened four days ago?

CASS. I wasn't going to tell you. But four days ago mum rang me at work. And in the course of a general discussion about nothing in particular, she asked when was I going to stop messing about with you, and make a serious effort to find – her words – 'one of your own'.

DAN. Josie actually said that?

CASS. I could hear dad in the background, so I was in no doubt she was speaking for both of them.

RONNIE. I don't believe you.

CASS. Don't blame her, Dan. *He* did it.

RONNIE. If that's true, you should both be grateful I flushed it out sooner rather than later.

CASS. *If* that's true?

DAN (*to* RONNIE). Why would you do that?

CASS. Because you wouldn't let him crawl back to his old room. Because you wouldn't let him turn back the clock to a time when his life was less poisoned by abject failure.

RONNIE. No offence, but you should see a psychiatrist.

CASS. No offence but you should see a whole fucking clinic. Coming back to England with your eye-witness accounts and your shocking reports.

RONNIE. I came back with the *Truth*.

CASS. The 'truth'? I've been reading up since your return.

RONNIE (*mocking*). Oh? You've been *reading*?

CASS. I wanted to find out what had turned my brother into a sour mouthpiece. Precisely which *truth* did you bring back exactly, Ronnie? There are literally hundreds. Shall we start with some Palestinian truths?

DAN. Cass –

CASS (*not to be stopped*). Which perspective would you like? The Palestinian people's? The Palestinian Authority's? The Palestinian National Council's? The Palestinian Legislative Council's? The Palestinian intellectuals'? The Palestinian

MPs? The Palestinian unions? The Palestinian Diaspora's? The PLO's? Or just Fatah's? Or the PFLP's? The DFLP's? Hamas? Islamic Jihad's? The Muslim Brotherhood's? Or shall we try someone else's truth now?

RONNIE. What I've been describing to mum and dad are things I saw with my own eyes.

CASS. It's not even *what* you're describing. It's *why* you are.

RONNIE. The White House handshake simply allows them sovereignty over their own misery.

CASS. It's what you seek to achieve by describing it.

RONNIE. A mockery of sovereignty for which they have to police their own dissidents –

CASS. *Dissidents*?!

RONNIE. – build settlements for American Zionists, have no right of return for refugees, and watch their unelected and corrupt representatives negotiate the Palestinian '*State*' into a series of smashed up, disconnected encampments, where freedom is relative, and cardinal resources like water, power and access are outside their control. This is actually happening.

CASS. Fanatics who blow themselves up in shopping centres aren't dissidents, Ronnie.

RONNIE. I'm talking about political dissidents. Lawyers. Academics. Doctors – not just fanatics.

CASS. They pack the bombs with nails so that if they don't kill outright they at least disfigure for life.

RONNIE. Repulsive and abhorrent, of course. But just like dad, you'll focus on the outrage of individual incidents rather than the broader reality of repression and resistance to repression going hand in hand. That each atrocity from whichever side is yet another step on the spiral of terror and counter-terror. That the spiral is downwards, into an ever-deepening pool of innocent blood – Jewish and Palestinian, pouring into each other until the distinction is no longer apparent, and it's all just thick, red, sickening blood.

CASS. Are you quoting from memory, or did you just make that up? No wonder dad got physical. Anything to stop you spouting like a badly-written pamphlet.

RONNIE. Dad hit me because I called him an anti-Semite.

CASS (*beat*). You called him what?

DAN. I think I've heard enough. I think you'd better leave.

RONNIE. He called me a self-hating Arab lover, so I called him a blinkered anti-Semite.

CASS. You called your own father an anti-Semite? Dad would never have told you to your face, but the day you boarded the plane for Tel Aviv was the proudest day of his life!

RONNIE. Mine too! Mine too! But I came to realise that anyone who supports the denial of basic human rights to the Palestinians is endorsing a situation whose outcome is always going to be more murdered Jews. It's not classical anti-Semitism, but in terms of the end result it may as well be. Millions of Israelis understand this – why not him?

CASS. Do you resent Dan and I so much you'll say just about *anything* to undermine us?

RONNIE. How self-obsessed are you? What's passing between me and them has nothing to do with you and Dan!

CASS. Don't insult my intelligence.

RONNIE. A letter from the West Bank was sent here. Dan passed it on to me. (*To* DAN.) Yes?

DAN. Yes.

CASS. After everything he's been trying to do to us, you're on his side now?

DAN. It's not about sides – it's about not losing the capacity to recognise something for what it actually is.

CASS. Oh I see what's happening. Ronnie and Danny ride again!

RONNIE. Dan gave me the letter. Mum found it cleaning my room. Showed it to dad. He claimed he wanted to understand.

I started to explain. But when he heard *what* I was explaining, boy did he not want to know. Start of rumpus, end of story. It's not about you. You're so crippled by your own inability to be definitive about a man you've only known for twenty years why would you need me to interfere?

DAN. But you did.

RONNIE. When I came back it seemed you two didn't know what you wanted from one another so yes, I thought maybe you needed a . . . a *catalyst* to force you together or put you out of your misery – I don't know.

DAN. So you could move back to your room.

RONNIE. Maybe moving back to my room was mixed up in it somewhere – I was straight off the plane from one war zone into another. Everything I was expecting to be the same had changed. I was looking around for some solid ground and I couldn't find a single patch.

CASS. Who was the letter from?

RONNIE. Letter?

CASS. From the West Bank.

RONNIE. From the brother of a woman I . . .

Pause.

CASS. You . . . ?

RONNIE. She doesn't fit into your awesome web of intrigue so it really doesn't matter.

CASS. A Palestinian woman?

RONNIE. No, the letter was written outside the territories but posted inside for the novelty postmark. What do you think?

CASS (*beat*). What's her name?

RONNIE. What do you care, Cass?

CASS. You had feelings for her?

RONNIE. What do you care?

CASS. You loved her?

RONNIE. Answer my question.

CASS. What's her name?

RONNIE (*beat*). Her name is. Her name *was* . . . Zahra.

CASS. Zara?

RONNIE. Za*h*ra.

CASS. Where did you meet?

RONNIE. What's the point?

CASS. I'm interested.

RONNIE (*beat*). She worked in a youth hostel I stayed at. We had a thing for about nine months, after which time I asked her to come back to the U.K. with me. Happy?

CASS. She didn't want to?

RONNIE. She couldn't leave her family. So I said I would stay with her – a suggestion she openly laughed at.

DAN. Why?

RONNIE. It made no sense to her that someone with the freedom to pursue his wildest ambitions would willingly consign himself to a life under occupation. But I insisted I was serious, until one morning she came to me and sat me down. She took my hands and told me to look into her eyes. And then in her most serious voice, she told me she was pregnant with my child.

DAN. Pregnant?

RONNIE. She wasn't. She knew it even as she said it.

DAN. Then why say it?

RONNIE. To read the eyes of her Jewish lover at the moment of truth. Empty promises litter the streets over there. She needed to test the veracity of mine.

CASS. And what did she read in your eyes?

RONNIE. What does it matter what she read?

CASS. It may be the last time the real you was spotted.

RONNIE. The real me?

CASS. What did Zahra read in your eyes at the moment of truth?

RONNIE (*beat*). *Maafee farah. Khawf faqat.*

DAN. In English?

RONNIE (*beat*). No joy. Only fear.

Pause.

CASS. And then what?

RONNIE. And then what?

CASS. And then what?

DAN (*beat*). There is no *and then what.* Isn't that right, Ronnie? Just Ben Gurion airport. Getting bumped up to Club Class. And home.

Pause.

CASS. How could you use people like that?

RONNIE. Use her? We had an affair. It didn't work out. It happens all the time.

CASS. I meant, when you came back. But possibly while you were there as well. Dear God . . .

RONNIE. What're you talking about?

CASS. Appropriating their struggle.

RONNIE. Appropriating?

CASS. Seeking association with the spirit of the underdog in the absence of any defining spirit of your own. Adopting the mantle of the aggrieved to avoid having to face that your own life has been without grief. Without pain. Without injustice. Without – in fact – any reason for its failure other than your own failings as a human being.

DAN (*gently*). Cassie . . .

RONNIE (*quiet*). The Palestinians have been shafted by everyone for over thirty years. They stand and watch as their land is clawed away from under their noses, while their leaders are either bought off, humiliated, held responsible for acts they have no way of stopping, or simply executed.

CASS. As Lou might say . . . yes, Ronnie, we *know*. But that's their struggle. Before we can be of any use to that, we have to sort out our own.

RONNIE *stands silently.*

Pause.

CASS *slowly crosses to him, and puts her arms around her brother, and holds him.* DAN *watches.*

After a few moments, HELEN *comes out onto the roof, holding a lighted cigarillo.*

HELEN. Um. I thought I'd better come up and let you know that Douglas and Louise are talking about going. I've tried persuading them to stay, but the coverage quickly boiled down to lots of excited people in cagoules pointing at the sky. I'm afraid there's a very real sense that the party's literally moved on.

DAN. I'll go down.

DAN *crosses to the entrance and goes downstairs.* HELEN *watches* DAN *exit.* RONNIE *breaks away from* CASS *and sits alone, upstage, watched by* CASS.

Pause. HELEN *approaches* CASS.

HELEN (*glancing at* RONNIE, *his head now in his hands*). Everything okay?

CASS (*looking at* RONNIE). I don't think he knows who he is anymore.

HELEN. And you?

CASS (*snapping out of it*). Thanks anyway.

HELEN. Thanks anyway?

CASS. Obviously if I'd've known Ronnie was going to come in like he did.

Beat.

Bit of a disaster all round. But perhaps it's for the best you weren't able to . . . you know.

HELEN. But I was.

CASS. When?

HELEN. When you sent him up with my glasses.

CASS. But you scarcely had time.

HELEN. You know what I'm like working to a deadline, Cassie. Given the circumstances I'd've been more than a little taken aback if his response had been immediate.

CASS. Of course.

HELEN. So you can imagine my surprise when I went for my cigarillos just now, and found this in my coat pocket.

HELEN *offers* CASS *a folded piece of notepaper. Beat.*

CASS *stares at the piece of paper.*

CASS. What is it?

HELEN. Pause.

CASS. I suddenly feel extremely sick.

HELEN. In the documentary at this point – I don't know if you remember, Cassie. At this point the clients were offered two choices. Not all of them did this, but the practitioner we shadowed offered two choices in recognition of the fact that some women – even when faced with overwhelming evidence of their partner's capacity for infidelity – some women will nevertheless choose to turn a blind eye.

CASS (*a wave of fear comes over her*). Oh Christ, Helen . . .

HELEN. She offered these choices to leave control with the client.

CASS. What's choice number one?

HELEN. Choice number one is I destroy this immediately and we pretend it never happened. The key word I'll emphasise is *pretend*.

CASS. Let me see it.

HELEN. Letting you see it is choice number two.

CASS. Give me the paper.

> CASS *holds out her hand. After a moment* HELEN *steps forward and places the piece of paper in* CASS*'s hand.*

HELEN. He must have slipped it into my pocket while I was begging some free tax advice from Douglas. Mind you. I did lay it on pretty thick. Sexual favours for complete career resurrection, so possibly not so difficult to resist for a thirty-five-year-old duffer going nowhere.

> CASS *opens the note and stares at it.*

CASS (*beat*). This isn't Dan's handwriting.

HELEN (*beat*). What?

CASS. This isn't Dan's handwriting.

HELEN. It must be.

CASS. This isn't the number of his mobile.

> LOU *comes out onto the roof, wearing her coat.*

LOU. Dan's very sweetly trying to get us to stay –

CASS. It's Doug's number.

> LOU *stops in her tracks.* CASS *looks up from the piece of paper.*

LOU (*beat*). What did you just say?

> CASS *instinctively screws up the piece of notepaper.*

What's that in your hand?

CASS. Nothing.

LOU (*beat*). Cass. In the twelve years we've known each other, have I ever previously struck you as a total fucking moron?

CASS. No.

LOU. So show me what's in your hand.

CASS (*beat*). No.

LOU. Show me what's in your hand.

CASS *shakes her head. They regard one another. Long pause.*

What the fuck's going on here?

HELEN. I offered to screw little Danny to determine if Cassie could completely trust him.

CASS. Helen . . .

HELEN. I just went for a cigarillo and discovered a piece of paper in my coat pocket, inscribed with a mobile number and the message, 'let's meet'.

CASS. Helen, don't!

HELEN. I assumed it was Dan, inviting me to call to arrange a rendezvous.

LOU. Cass?

HELEN. I assumed wrong.

DAN *now enters.*

DAN. I tried bribing Doug with unlimited access to the telescope, but he seems pretty set on –

DAN *picks up the atmosphere on the roof and stops talking. He regards the three women on the roof. After a moment* DOUGLAS *comes onto the roof in his jacket.*

DOUGLAS. I told him we couldn't be so easily bought.

DOUGLAS *crosses to* LOU *and gently kisses the nape of her neck. She doesn't respond, looking directly at* CASS *all the time.*

We should be making a move.

DOUGLAS *is suddenly aware of the atmosphere on the roof.* LOU *stands frozen, facing* CASS.

Long pause.

LOU. After what you've just seen. Do you trust yours any more, or any less? You think he's one thing, Cass. And he is. But he's also other things. Do you think this is the first time?

CASS. But you and Douglas are . . . you're Lou and Douglas.

LOU. Unfortunately my husband has a weakness for fuckable stupidity. We try not to broadcast it.

HELEN. Hey! *Bitch!*

LOU. Being married is no guarantee, Cass. Having children is no guarantee. There are no guarantees. (*Pointing at* HELEN.) So if this vacuous fake has sold you one, I'd ask for your money back.

HELEN (*offended*). How fucking dare you? No-one's being paid here.

LOU (*facing* HELEN). You mean . . . you do this for *free*?

DAN. I'm sorry, but did I miss something when it all went dark?

DOUGLAS (*beat, subdued*). I'm . . . I'll go down to the car.

LOU. Do that.

DOUGLAS (*pathetically brave face*). It's taking longer to start every time.

DAN (*trying to help him out*). Have you checked the battery?

DOUGLAS. In summer?

DAN. Average lifespan is approximately three years, regardless.

DOUGLAS. I didn't know that.

DAN. Most die in winter because usage is that much heavier.

DOUGLAS. Of course. Heaters, demisters, wipers, headlights, starting up from frozen –

LOU (*sharp, not looking at him*). Douglas.

DOUGLAS *stops his litany. Beat.*

DAN. Bring chummy over one night when I've got Oscar round. Point them at the sky. Blow two tiny minds for the price of one.

DOUGLAS. I'd like that. Well.

Beat.

Thanks, Cass.

CASS. Doug.

DAN. I'll see you to the door.

DOUGLAS (*to* LOU). I'll wait for you downstairs.

LOU. Yes.

DOUGLAS *hesitates for a moment.*

DOUGLAS. Lou –

LOU (*cutting him off*). Not here.

DOUGLAS (*beat*). No.

DOUGLAS *makes a wide berth of* HELEN *and goes back downstairs, followed by* DAN. *Beat.*

CASS. I'm so sorry.

LOU. Stop asking how is it all going to end before it's even begun. Stop living in uncertainty, start living *with* it. My relationship with Douglas is an open-ended condition. I accept that because the alternative is unacceptable.

HELEN. I'm sorry but that is such bollocks.

LOU (*pointing again at* HELEN). The alternative is to become a lethal little zealot like your boss here. Cynically squinting at the world from inside her Prada bunker. Be brave, Cass. Build on the past, don't be a slave to it. Move forward. (*Kissing* CASS *on the cheek.*) God bless.

LOU *exits downstairs. Pause.*

HELEN. If my self-esteem ever sank that low I hope I'd at least have the dignity to drown myself.

CASS (*beat*). I'll see you at the office in the morning.

HELEN (*looking at* RONNIE). I'm not going to get the treatment, am I?

CASS. I don't think so, no.

HELEN. Whatever he's been paid, *I want back.*

ACT TWO 95

Beat.

See myself out.

CASS *lets out a long, deep breath, the tension finally leaving her.* DAN *comes onto the roof.*

DAN. I know you think the sun shines out of that woman's –

CASS. Hold me.

DAN *stops, hesitates for a moment, and crosses over to* CASS, *taking her in his arms. They hold one another, clinging on for dear life.*

Pause.

I'm so sorry.

DAN. I'm burning my films.

CASS. I am so so sorry.

DAN. I can't offer you more than you're holding right now. You have to decide if that's enough.

CASS *pulls him tighter to her. The telephone rings downstairs.*

CASS (*beat*). I'll go.

DAN. *I'll* go. The answerphone picks up after six rings.

CASS (*crossing to the entrance*). Then I'd better get used to it.

CASS *goes downstairs.* DAN *watches her.*

Pause.

After a moment he turns to RONNIE.

DAN. The letter, Ronnie. What did it say?

RONNIE. It asked me that whatever happened, not to forget them.

DAN (*beat*). If I receive any more, where shall I send them?

RONNIE (*beat*). I don't know.

Long pause.

What now, Dan? What now?

DAN. Ask Raoul. He was never short of a plan.

RONNIE (*looking up*). Raoul's gone.

DAN. Well, then. I guess you're on your own.

DAN and RONNIE regard one another as CASS appears at the entrance to the roof.

DAN slowly turns away from RONNIE, and faces CASS.

CASS. It was mum. Asking if I'd heard from Ronnie.

DAN. What did you tell her?

CASS. I said he *was* here. But then he went.

CASS holds out her hand. DAN crosses to the entrance and takes it. She kisses his hand and leads him downstairs.

RONNIE looks ahead as the sounds of London rise. After a moment the sounds of Hebron rise in competition – a muezzin* calling the faithful to prayer, and the thok-thok of a helicopter gunship overhead. The noise rises in volume, as RONNIE covers his ears with his hands.

Slow fade to black.

End.

---

* *muezzin* – the official of a mosque responsible for calling the faithful to prayer.